Shoeleather and the Bayonet

Steven L. Acker

To Frank,
Thank too far
helping me tell the Start

Orange Hat Publishing
www.orangehatpublishing.com - Waukesha, WI

For information, please contact:

Orange Hat Publishing
www.orangehatpublishing.com
603 N Grand Ave, Waukesha, WI 53186

Edited by Denise Guibord
Cover art and design by Julia Gueller

www.orangehatpublishing.com

To Linda

Chapter One

April 2ⁿᵈ, 1862

In a sea of confederate canvas, Hiram Stringer navigates the myriad of regiments looking for one specific company, the unit of his former college roommate. Finding the right regiment and the right company, he moves between two even rows of white tents looking for the man in charge— the first sergeant. Among a company street of men dressed in the same homespun uniform of blue overshirt with red cuffs and collar atop civilian pants of jean cloth, Hiram's professionally tailored uniform of grey satinet makes him look like what he is: the son of affluence and privilege. Curious eyes watch as Hiram moves to a sturdy looking man of about thirty who's writing a letter. Looking down, Hiram sees a carte-de-visite of a young woman of around twenty, perched so the writer can look upon the image as he writes. The man with sergeant's stripes feels the sun blocked from his letter. Looking up, he sees Hiram.

"What business do you have?" Orderly Sergeant George Stewart inquires.

Hiram passes a piece of paper to Stewart, "I'm in your company."

Standing up, Stewart inspects the impeccably dressed new recruit down to his knapsack. He admires the perfectly made kepi sitting rakishly over Hiram's black wavy hair.

"Your captain said to add me to your rolls."

Stewart reads the orders, "Hiram Stringer. Says here, you're transferring from the University Grays. University Grays?"

"Yes, sergeant. University of Mississippi. Only four of the hundred and thirty-five of us didn't enlist, most of us in the Grey's," Hiram beams.

"Then why you joining us?"

A new man arrives. Tucker Current, seeing an opportunity for his kind of fun, attends the meeting of Highland, Mississippi, and the fine bred Hiram. "Who's this snappy pants, George, I mean, sergeant?"

With a dismissive wave of his hand toward Tucker, Stewart returns to Hiram Stringer. "Why would you leave your college classmates for this company of hickories?" Stewart motions to a street full of tawny men built from farm labor, each of them wearing wide-brimmed hats from home.

Hiram can clearly see the difference between his veranda summers and the men around him, and he begins to question his decision, but then commits to it. "I have a friend in this company."

By now a gaggle of the curious surround Hiram, each

fascinated by the uniform and the man.

"Son, nobody in Highland gone anywhere near a college," Stewart pauses as he remembers, "except maybe Miller."

Tucker joins in, "Yea, Miller went to some fancy school in Oxford, I think, but he wern't there but a couple a months before he quit and ran home."

"Three months, and he didn't quit." Hiram begins to defend his friend. "He's not the quitting sort," an accusation he's sure Clay would not like.

"Settle yerself," Stewart returns. Turning to Tucker, "Miller don't quit, believe me, he don't quit even when he should."

"Like sniffin fer Julie." In a small town everyone knows everyone's business. Julie is Sergeant Stewart's wife and Clay Miller is in love with her.

"Shut up, Tucker."

Growing impatient with such pedestrian gobbledygook, Hiram looks around for Clay. Not seeing him, he turns to Stewart, "Don't seem to be able to locate him amongst this collection of monochromatics."

Tucker riles at the big word tossed out, assuredly an insult. He postures as though offended at this attack on his honor. Tucker moves in, "Monochrom what?"

Before he can land hell on Hiram, Stewart interjects, "One color is all he's saying. One color, as in blue."

Tucker and the rest relax at the realization that the perceived slight is actually an accurate description. Bored with the new man, they return to their camp life, leaving Stewart and Hiram alone.

"Where is he?" Hiram returns Stewart to the topic at hand.

"You sure he's worth it? Not too late to rejoin your unit," Stewart says. "We don't take kindly to strangers, especially if we feel they are our betters. And son, you dress our better."

"Only cloth and tailoring, sergeant." He knows Clay is cut from the same cloth as those surrounding him.

"Fair enough. Just remember, Clay's Highland folk, so don't be surprised at how he takes seeing you."

"Where is he?"

"I figured we'd need some extra rations for the boys before we have a go at the Yankees so I sent Tucker's brother and your boy to town." Stewart returns to his letter, leaving Hiram standing alone.

Chapter Two

Alex Current and Clay Miller move through Corinth, a railroad town, built barely six years prior. All roads lead to the Tishomingo Hotel, a two-story, wood-faced hotel with a wide porch on each floor. Crossing the tracks in front of the hotel, they enter a human circus of vendors plying their wares. Jugglers entertain for a penny while vendors sell everything from pipes to clothing. Clay sees a tinsmith.

"Over there Alex," Clay points to the tinsmith.

Alex, a powerful twenty-year-old with a broad chest and stout limbs, moves people out of the way as he pushes through the crowd. In his wake, Clay Miller, also twenty, with a long athletic body, navigates the crowds using apologetic gestures. Arriving at the tinsmith, Clay acquires a brand new tin cup.

"Lookie there, Clay," Alex points toward the side of the hotel where a grizzled man wearing a full-length linen duster sells.

"He's got what we need."

"Food?"

"No." Alex points to the alley. "Look."

Behind the duster man, two young black women, bare shouldered enough to excite the imagination, invite the eye of passing soldiers. The more robust one makes eye contact with Alex as he moves closer. The petite one gives Clay a side glance as her pursed lips separate slightly. Clay is a virgin to human intimacy. He begins to turn away.

"Clay, ya gotta stand for somethin in this world," Highland's strongest man tells his best friend. "And I could stand for some of that."

The duster man, seeing a potential customer running away, envelops Clay with his beefy arm. "She likes you, boy." Turning to the slight girl, he winks at her in a practiced sales technique. "Don't ya, girlie?"

"Sure do." She smiles at Clay. "You pretty for a white boy."

"Alex!" Clay calls out like a shy boy in a man's world.

"It's okay, Clay." Alex pulls the beefy arm from his friend. "Mister, I'll take both of them."

Alex turns to Clay to hand him the money Stewart gave them for the extra rations. Clay watches Alex disappear in the alley next to the hotel. Alone, he looks about nervously. The sounds and chaos of a city intimidate him. He saw a bit of the world when he went to college, but that was a refined version, not the tobacco spitting, guttural world currently surrounding him. Not sure what to do, Clay stands in an eddy of humanity wishing he were invisible, and feeling like he is.

"Young fella," the beefy arm returns. "I know my girls, and I'm here to tell ya, your pard will be busy for some time."

Clay's heart sinks as he begins to feel the suffocation of someone too close to him.

"Is there something else you need, seein that female contact ain't it? Hungry maybe?"

Clay's mind returns to the reason he's in town, "We were sent her to get extra food for our company." Clay feels the beefy arm tighten around his shoulders.

"I believe I have just the thing. I bet your boys would really enjoy some sausage. Smoked in hickory, ready to eat, and the best in Corinth if I say so myself. Had some for supper last night."

Excited by the idea, "Sausage would do fine, mister."

"That'll be twenty dollars for a full sack. Pay me now and I'll run and get it for ya."

The company gave Alex fourteen dollars. Seeing Clay's face, duster man changes his tack. "How much ya got?"

"Fourteen dollars, Bank of Natchez money."

Making a dramatic inspection of the young man like his countenance is the application for a bank loan, duster man acts out the evaluation of Clay's character.

Nodding, he finalizes the plan. "Well, son. You look an honest sort, and the boys need their sustenance if they're goin to whip the Yankees. By Jimmies, I'll make this deal with you, the hardest deal I've made all day."

The vendor squeezes Clay's shoulders more. "Give me

the fourteen and I'll run down the alley and get them sausages for ya." Exchange made, he disappears down the alley leaving Clay standing alone in a sea of dark humanity.

Chapter Three

For an hour Hiram waits for Clay to return. Alone, and mostly ignored except as a curiosity, Hiram watches the men of Clay's hometown. Of various heights and builds, ages from mid teen to well past forty, he listens to their folksy banter in order to understand the fabric of the men he will serve with, to compare them to the company he first joined. The University Greys, the student body of the University of Mississippi, held host to the best families of the state. Eloquent and fiery in their determination to protect their chattel institutions, they acted like crusaders setting out to free the Holy Land. By the looks of Highland's slouch hats and boots, these men are mostly hardscrabble farmers, too poor to own a slave even if they wanted to. Glad to be away from the zealots of slavery, Hiram also understands that small towns are clannish in their acceptance of strangers, especially strangers of the ilk Hiram carries in his kit and upbringing. Hiram continues to look for Clay.

Instead, he sees Tucker returning. "Know what they call a pretty girl in Highland?" Tucker says.

"No," Hiram humors the moment.

"A visitor." Tucker laughs at his own joke when something over Hiram's shoulder draws his attention. "There's my brother."

Both men look down the street where Hiram sees a large, brutish young man coming toward them. Alex stops in the middle of the company street in order to draw a crowd for his story.

"There I was with not one, but two ladies, naked as jaybirds, just about to do our business, when their handler comes in and scoots them out of the tent. Before I had a chance to protest, he had a derringer pressed against my face. Said, I was done. 'Mister,' I said." Alex mimics himself, "'I guess I am.' And off they went."

Tucker and the others laugh with Alex, not at him. It's here Alex notices the well dressed oddity standing next to his brother.

"Didn't even dip my wick." Alex moves toward the stranger. "Maybe you'll do for a poke." Laughter intensifies as Hiram stands in the path of Alex's idea of wit.

Tucker moves to Hiram, "Brother, this is our new recruit. Came to us from some college. Came to us to be with his friend."

Stewart explains, "He came to us to be with Miller."

"Oh shit, I forgot him." Alex starts back to town, but pauses at the idea of his best friend having another friend. "You know Clay?"

"Yes, from college. He was my roommate."

"Odd, he never mentioned you." Alex has been Clay's only real friend since they were kids.

"Never mentioned you either," Hiram responds sharply.

Alex looks, surprised. Everyone retreats from Alex. Standing proudly, Alex announces, "Clay Miller's my best friend."

"Then why did you leave him?"

Alex moves in to rain hell on Hiram, when, for the second time today, Stewart interjects to avoid the potential hassle. "Alex, go retrieve Miller before he gets himself killed, or worse, loses our money?" With a mischievous smile he stirs the pot, "Take this one with you."

"No."

The setting sun further darkens the alley Clay has stared into for an hour. Dark characters and irrational thoughts have moved in and out of that alley all day, but no duster man or Alex. Like rats coming out at night, the alley begins divulging its night creatures. Rough men, with mean faces, glare at the fresh-faced boy standing at the edge of their world while Clay stands inert, not able to enter an alley where he may find Alex dead, or a knife waiting to kill him. Afraid to return to camp empty handed and more afraid of going into the darkness, fear grows The night creatures smell that fear. Two of them move in.

A bearded ghoul approaches from the front, "Sonny, you bouts to have a bad night."

The other one moves behind Clay, "Easier ifn ya don't fight. Die quicker and quieter."

A knife aims at Clay. Where one man would fight. Where another would run. Where yet another might cry for help, he stands completely still. The knife begins its movement forward. Clay clenches his teeth. He closes his eyes. A frozen moment waiting for death. Instead of the feeling of the blade, he hears a grunt then a thump. Opening his eyes, he sees Alex smashing the bearded face into a bloody pulp. The other runs into the darkness.

"Let's get you back."

"I lost the money."

"I know."

Alex brings Clay back to camp where he tells everyone that Clay was robbed. Hiram comes up to his friend. Clay's defeated face illuminates for a moment when Alex interposes, "Clay, check out this peacock. Ain't he pretty?"

Caught between Alex and Hiram, Clay turns his back on Hiram. *Two worlds should never meet.*

A bugle calls the camp to bed. Stewart orders, "We move out in a couple of hours. Stringer, you're with me."

April 3rd, 1862

A sliver of Eastern light illuminates General Albert Sidney Johnston's army preparing for its march North. Along the company street, each man in Clay's company packs his gear for this first real march of their army career. In small gunny sacks, knapsacks, and blanket rolls, men pack creature comforts they deem indispensable. Razor, towel, soap, too many shirts, a slew of socks, Bible, rope, comb, etc, each man overloads himself. Only the poor are immune from the decision of what to bring. Clay has a simple blanket roll wrapped over his shoulder, inside an extra shirt and pair of socks. Already packed, and not seeing Alex anywhere, Clay looks to Hiram.

In front of Stewart's tent, Hiram has his personals laid out neatly: a rubberized raincoat, two blankets, two shirts, three pair of socks, writing desk, soap, towel, shaving kit, and a full poke bag. Clay watches Hiram evaluate each item for its weight and its worth: extra blanket finds the mud, razor finds the knapsack, extra shirt goes in the knapsack, and so it continues until a small pile of extra goods deemed not worth the weight sits next to a knapsack full to the bulge. From a large cotton poke sack Hiram pulls out two leather bound volumes. Clay draws nearer to see the titles, an action noticed by Hiram.

"Do you want these?

"What are they?" Clay moves closer, not just for the titles, but to be near his friend.

"*Dante's Inferno* and a bit of the darkness of Hawthorne." Hiram holds them up for Clay to see, "If you remember, two of my favorites."

Just as Clay declines the books, Alex's meaty hand reaches in. Thumbing through the pages in caricatured dramatics, farcical facial expressions parody the pages Alex skims. Like an actor entering the stage, Alex draws himself up so all can see him as he begins his show.

"Good book?" Alex asks as he finds an illustration of the levels of hell. He laughs at the third level of hell. "Gluttony ain't one I'll be livin in any time soon."

"Thanks to Clay, that is," Tucker yelps.

"Shut up, Tucker."

Seeing a glimmer of intelligent conversation in the brutish lout, Hiram warms to Alex. "Yes. Yes, it is. Too bad gluttony will not join us on our journey."

"Good to wipe my ass with," Alex laughs as he tears out a good supply. "Who needs some," he offers the book up high for all to see. The company roars. Clay's stomach tightens.

"I've got the quick step coming out my ass somethin fierce," Tucker rips out a chapter.

Hiram begins to protest when others line up. Bad water, bad hygiene, and poor rations since they arrived at Corinth has almost the entire company suffering from dysentery. Hiram knows what fights are better left unfought. And so it goes until all that remains are a few odd pages precariously attached to the battered cover.

"At least it went to some good," Hiram philosophizes, a comment that draws a good-natured laugh from Stewart and some others.

"Here, Clay," Alex offers the remnants. Clay too suffers from diarrhea.

Caught betwixt and between, Clay freezes for a moment.

December 1860

Freshman year of college and Clay returns to the small room he shares with a junior student. He plops his homework on the table next to Hiram Stringer's favorite volumes, the themes of the two topics speak volumes as to the men sharing the room.

Hiram smiles at the title, "Emerson I see. Too optimistic for me. Dante is much better suited to our times."

Hiram was sent to college to master the classics required of the social elite, so he spends his academic hours reading Greek tragedies and modern compositions while his personal hours, to his father's approval, has Hiram learning about those not as privileged as he. Coming from a long line of freethinkers, Hiram lived in one of the few homes with free black help. Mr. Stringer even taught his charges how to read, and while neighbors swore the Stringer home was a stop in the Underground Railroad, no one could prove it. Besides, Mr. Stringer's position as an acclaimed doctor kept the locals from shunning a man whose services they needed. As an upperclassman, Hiram had the power to select his roommate. Dr. Stringer calls those without a veranda the fabric of the culture, and Hiram has chosen to learn about that fabric by living with a boy with dirt under his fingernails. Hiram is polished cotton and silk. Clay is jean cloth. Hiram studies with an ease born from privilege and practice while Clay puts shoulder to plow every night.

Plant the seed, tend the plant, in order to harvest the

crop. That's the approach Clay takes to learning. He commits every word spoken by his professor to paper, tending those words like seedlings. Each evening's reading acts as the sun and rain to ideas born in class. And all too often Clay finishes the night more confused than when he started. Yet he hasn't quit his studies just like a farmer doesn't quit his fields. Every night Clay buries his mind in ideas new to him. Tonight is no different.

"I see you're reading transcendentalism," Hiram observes a complex philosophy in the hands of his roommate.

"This one nearly killed the cow," Clay digs into his notes. "Listen to this." He reads:

'The belief that individual virtue and happiness depend upon self-realization – this depends upon the reconciliation of two universal psychological tendencies:

a. the expansive or self-transcending tendency - a desire to embrace the whole world - to know and become one with the world.

b. the contracting or self-asserting tendency - the desire to withdraw, remain unique and separate - an egotistical existence.'

"'What the hell does that mean? Reconciliation. Expansive. Contracting. Existence!" Clay pushes the notes away. Farms do fail and a broken back is often the harvest of effort. Hiram can sense his roommate begin to dance with quitting.

"I can't do this anymore," Clay's voice resigns itself. Struggling to stay afloat, grabbing onto anything his mind can control, Clay thinks of returning home. "Some fields ain't

meant to be plowed," Clay closes his notes. Highland. The farm. He weighs physical pain of that place to mental anguish of his mind trying to understand Transcendentalism. He blurts out, "Working the woodlot ain't a bad way to spend the day."

From the first day, Hiram has seen a natural intelligence in the young man from the country. Clay has a genuine thirst to learn, something Hiram seldom sees among the stayed social elites at the university. Seeing Clay's taut face, Hiram decides sometimes even the best horse needs a pull of the reins.

"My father and I attended a lyceum in New Orleans where Mr. Emerson spoke on his efforts at Brook Farm. My father considers Emerson the brightest mind of this century." Hiram moves Clay's homework to the center of the table then offers, "Let me help you."

Clay reluctantly takes the remaining pages from the gloating Alex.

"It was a shitty book anyway," Hiram's commoner word choice lightens the mood and disperses the crowd. Temporarily disarmed by the wit of his rival, Alex moves away leaving Clay standing awkwardly next to Hiram for a moment uncomfortable for one, delicious for another. Eager to get away from the tension, Clay begins to move away when Hiram calls his attention.

"Clay, what do you think of this?"

Reaching into the poke bag, Hiram pulls out a twin of the kepi he's wearing. Clay instantly wants the kepi and begins to reach for it when Hiram pulls away. Beyond Clay's reach now, Hiram inspects the polished visor and satinet lines of the French inspired kepi so Clay can see its quality. In an army of civilian hats, the kepi stands out as just about the only semblance of a uniform. Hiram extends his laden hand toward Clay. Clay moves toward the kepi.

"Think Sergeant Stewart will like this?" Hiram's payback.

Before Clay can respond, the gift is given and a hearty handshake is shared between Stewart and Hiram. Stewart proudly puts his kepi on for all to see, and then orders the company to fall in. In the shuffle to form the company, tall men move to the right while shorter men step to the left. Alex and Clay fall in on the right, Hiram near the middle. Clay looks to the kepi that was supposed to be his then looks down the line at his college friend, then to Alex.

January 1858

Buried under too few blankets, Clay pulls them over his head so he can use his breath for heat. Curled up as small as possible, he stares into darkness as the sounds of another violent fight fills the downstairs of the small country home. A bottle broken against a wall startles Clay. Moments later, a dull thud makes him sit up. Turning his ear to the doorway, he hears tormenting words lording over his fallen mother. Clay pulls himself from bed. No longer noticing the cold, he moves to the stairs and looks down to the yellow candlelight. His ears strain. Almost imperceptible. Muffled. Gurgled. He hears, ever so faintly, so labored, his name. Without thought, he sprints down the stairs and into the kitchen where he sees Mr. Miller hunched over the prostrate form of Clay's mother. Mr. Miller's finger dig deep into her neck. She gurgles. She sees her son. She mouths words. Clay launches himself at Mr. Miller, knocking the smallish man to the floor. A coughing sound draws Clay to his mother. Kneeling next to her, he sees the red lines where Mr. Miller's fingers choked.

"I'm okay, son." His mother reassures.

Immediately, Clay feels the heat of Mr. Miller's breath as he lands on the boy's back. In the struggle between the teenage boy and his stepfather, the battle is unequal. Clay is stronger than Miller, but Mr. Miller holds the real power, the power built from unending abuse, of position in the hierarchy of family. Clay has the physical strength to kill the old man, but he doesn't for reasons he doesn't understand. Clay wishes he were angry. He isn't. He wishes he could defend himself. He can't. Mr. Miller is not bound by such calm. Raging at the idea of the boy touching him and celebrating the opportunity to raise the ante, he moves nose to nose with Clay.

"Stand up, boy," Mr. Miller orders. Clay does as he's told. "Well, you're the man now. Ain't ya?" A powerful slap across Clay's face is meant to emasculate the boy. It works.

"Can't hide behind your mama's skirt now, can ya?" Clay can smell the whiskey. "You a man now. Facing yer pa like you just did." A full drawn slap. He repeats himself, "You think you're a real man now, don't ya?" Clay stands silent. "Take your medicine, boy." Mr. Miller puts his full force behind a punch to Clay's stomach. "I said, be still, boy."

Clay only fights for air..

A flurry of hard slaps right, then left, then right, then left pummels Clay with pain. Not physical pain as much as questioning pain.

Exhausted but still not satisfied, Mr. Miller heads toward the cupboard where he digs frantically tearing plates and dishes out of the way.

"Where the hell is it?"

Clay's mother hid Mr. Miller's pistol while he was beating the boy.

"Where'd ya put it? Never you mind, this will do the trick."
Mr. Miller pulls a knife from the drawer.

The point of the knife at a boy trained not to run. A thick arm coils. The boy closes his eyes. An inner voice tells Clay it will be over soon. A mother cries for help. White hands knock the drunk man to the floor where he passes out. Black hands pull the boy outside to sleep the night in a slave cabin. At first sound, Frank had run to Alex's house to get Old Man Current to help again. The next morning Mr. Miller awakens from the floor not sure how he got there and why breakfast isn't made. Supper that day was quiet except for Mr. Miller's questioning comments about the bruising on Clay's face.

April 6th, 1862

Last night, while Yankees slept under canvas, Confederate General Johnston skillfully brought his army of ill prepared men, undetected, to within yards of the

Yankee camps. This morning, Yankees snores drown out Rebel sergeants fighting to keep the element of surprise.

"Get up," Sergeant Stewart whispers to his corporals, then they do the same to the privates. Stiff bodies rise like old men. As Tucker and Alex head to a far-off tree to relieve themselves, Clay sneaks over to Hiram. He needs to say something to Hiram, not sure what, but he knows he needs to. Looking to the tree Hiram leaned against last night, Alex sees him fast asleep, his arms crossed and his head dipped deep into his chest. Clay pauses trying to decide how to apologize.

"Wake him too," says a passing Stewart.

The snap of a distant musket, quickly followed by a gunpowder reply, wakes Hiram. All eyes look to the direction of the noise. At first, the gunfire sounds like a few hunters on a coon hunt, then a peel of gunpowder thunder fills the soldiers with an ominous dread. Boom.

"What was that?" asks a shivering son of Mississippi.

"Cannon," responds a Mexican War veteran. Tension grows in the actions of the men as the voices of the officers and sergeants become more demonstrative.

Before Clay can speak, the company is ordered to fall in.

"Light marching order," Clay's captain says while fighting to put on an air of bravery, an effort betrayed by his trembling hands and cracking voice.

"You heard the captain," Sergeant Stewart reminds the men, "that means canteens and haversacks only. No blanket rolls or knapsacks. Make a pile." With a laugh he tells them, "And don't forget your muskets."

A few laughs tell Stewart he hasn't completely lost his men to fear. Clay returns to his blanket roll when Hiram calls him back.

"Clay," he offers in a grave voice. "I need you to take something for me."

Before Clay can check where Alex is, Hiram hands him a cloth poke sack. He's off before Clay can respond. Checking to see if anyone saw the exchange yet curious to see what's inside, another kepi maybe or a book, Clay opens the sack. He finds two copies of his favorite memory of college. His hands caress the titles. His favorite subject of his favorite time in life. Ralph Waldo Emerson. Henry David Thoreau. Inside these titles are the rhetoric for the mind that so filled Clay. Suddenly, deeply rutted hands rip Clay back to this world.

"'*The Dial: Literature, Philosophy Religion.*' I know where these came from," Alex speaks just loud enough for Clay to hear. He returns them to Clay, then, pausing for just a moment, his jealous face morphs into a mischievous one. Rising up, Alex calls loud enough to compete with a circus master, "Clay, tar me off a page or two just in case the quickstep comes back ta haunt me," Alex draws a crowd again.

Caught between betwixt and between, Clay does his best to placate Alex yet save Emerson. "Hang there while I find the softest pages."

Clay turns page after page in an exaggerated motion of testing softness hoping those around him will think he's trying to decide which essay will treat his ass the best. "Fate" comes out in jagged edges too close to the words, then a portion of "Nature." He desperately searches for the one essay he must have. It was the one essay of Emerson that he and Hiram found the most pleasure in—the most truth in. *Where is it?* Tossing one journal to Alex, he rips into the other.

Quickly he turns to the table of contents, an action Alex notices. "You gotta look up which ones to wipe with? That's queer."

Clay fumbles through the pages aware he's becoming a spectacle. He quickly tears out a chunk hoping "Self Reliance" is in there.

"There ya go, Alex, wipe away."

Emerson soon to be stained, the regiment forms, and Clay stuffs what he was able to save into the poke sack then into his haversack.

"Attention Battalion," booms the voice of their colonel. The regiment straightens. The throaty cheer of Mississippi men joins the sound of cannon and musket.

"Time to see the elephant, boys," informs a Mexican War veteran.

"What does that mean?" a virgin voice cries out.

Chapter Four

April 6th, 1862

Two ranks, each thirteen inches from the other. The few veterans of the Mexican War, or of the fight against the Seminoles, tighten their belts and bring their cartridge box to the front. They know what awaits. Tucker drains his canteen to still a dry mouth that has antagonized him since he heard the first shot. His canteen drained, he tosses it aside. Hiram Stringer appears to be praying, an action not lost on Alex.

"Your boy's a Christian. Well, that's somethin I guess." Alex nods.

Before Clay thinks about the ramifications of his next words on Hiram, he tells Alex, "He's Jewish."

Spitting out an egg-size chaw of tobacco, "Well, don't that beat all?"

"Quiet in the ranks," Stewart scolds.

In a company of introspective eyes, only one pair darts about in an external search. In spite of the military bearing of the moment, Clay's mind searches for an escape, not from the fear that fills most men's souls, but from a bodily function that threatens to explode.

Sergeant Stewart glares at the squirming private. "Miller, stand at attention," an order unregistering in a young man debating between wetting himself on the spot or breaking ranks. The growing pain has Clay seriously contemplating letting it all go. His head swivels one more time in a vain attempt to find relief only to discover his colonel searching for someone, and Clay's actions draws attention. Mounted on a huge bay, the colonel halts right in front of Private Miller. Clay stiffens. The colonel turns to the Clay's captain.

"Captain Parker, we need a man for the color guard." He points to Clay. "Have this man report."

Clay leaves the ranks to join the color guard by way of a nearby tree where his moment of physical relief gives him pause to swallow the grand significance and honor of joining the Color Guard; they are nine of the bravest men charged with the protection of a regimental flag. The men of the regiment see the flag as their identity—their pride. And the 7th has a beautiful scarlet flag, crisp and unstained, sewn by the ladies of Highland, including Julie, and entrusted to the color guard for its protection. Clay is about to become one of them.

Sprinting to the center of the regiment, Clay immediately notices the military bearing of the eight men with the flag. All of them are in kepis and most have full uniforms of gray. Some of them have first-rate muskets complete with bayonets. Clay has an old smoothbore converted to percussion, but he does have a bayonet. He almost had a kepi.

Stopping in front of them, he recognizes Sergeant Dix, a regular army sort who fought in the Seminole War, and now carries the flag. He wears his service like a bayonet. Dix moved to Highland after the war where he became deacon of Clay's church—a man bent on fire and brimstone. Next to him stands a man who was heading to West Point, if the war hadn't started when it did. And now Clay Miller proudly joins them. *Does the colonel see something in me?* Clay ponders. *Am I brave?*

"Sergeant Dix, take this one." The colonel impatiently orders. "He'll have to do until Cousin Charles returns from his chicken pox."

Dix turns to the crestfallen boy, "You, move to second rank behind me." Shaded by the Saint Andrew's cross on a red field, the small spark of pride born from misinterpreting a moment disappears in the quiet folds of cotton and batting.

Silence no longer the watchword, the colonel orders, "Attention Battalion!" in a stentorian voice that shakes the very forest. "Fix Bayonets," brings forth the sound of hundreds of bayonets fixing to muskets. Clay's bayonet goes on smoothly, and as quickly as Dix's. Pride whispers, *well done.*

"Shoulder, Arms!" Muskets move to the right shoulder

"Time to see the elephant," Dix tells his new charge.

"What's that?" Clay has never seen an elephant. "We got elephants?"

"No!" Dix scorns. "Cold steel. Combat. A bayonet charge."

"Port Arms!" Muskets go diagonally across the chest, the musket held tight by white knuckled hands. Clay goes to port arms.

"No, damned it. Color guard stays at the shoulder," barks Dix.

Turning his attention to the world around him, Clay becomes consumed in the moment. He looks down at the fine English shoes worn by the West Pointer, a prize given to the best shots in the regiment and every member of the color guard; Clay wears work boots still stained with the shit of his farm.

"Damn it, Miller," Sergeant Dix drives his fist into Clay's chest. "Go to the shoulder or I'll drive a bayonet up your ass."

"Battalion, Forward," The colonel points his sword.

The first rank of the color guard advance six paces. Dix and his flag will lead the charge by stepping six paces in front of the regiment. Clay's rank steps up one rank to fill the space left by Dix and the colors.

West Point gently explains, "The regiment guides on the colors. That's why they're out there and we're here." His voice offers more support than Dix's did.

In the front rank, the intensity electrifies Clay's body with a charge of energy built by thousands of human spirits about to take the same left step, at exactly the same time. The transcendentalism of it all does not escape him. He and Hiram spent many a night discussing the possibility of all men being interconnected by a life force, an Oversoul. When Clay packed for war, he made sure to bring a notebook of the transcendental concepts that most challenged his awareness of the world he lives in. The idea of an Oversoul connecting all human beings sounds beautiful on one level, but absurd on another. To be a part of something bigger than tending farm animals feels purposeful. To be connected to Mr. Miller sends bile through Clay. Hiram added another layer of thought when he told Clay, "If we are all interconnected, then we lose our ability to be unique and independent in a world bent on destroying itself." Hiram philosophized that being a strong individual is the only way a man can self-actualize—to meet his potential. Hiram's searing logic didn't fit life on the Miller farm.

War. Battle. Clay has his first sense of a universal movement of mankind. As he stands amid thousands, he feels his individuality meld into a single consciousness, an energy growing from men's souls through his own soul. He feels his Power grow.

"Guide Center," the colonel barks.

Bodies tense in a forward lean.

"March!" left feet step forward.

A spontaneous explosion of screams fills the air; a shrill yip followed by a banshee tenor rips through the morning air. The Rebel Yell. Drums blast a quick cadence. Clay's left is quickly followed by his right. Each step is an attack. Each step is a statement. A bullet whizzing overhead goes unnoticed, drowned out by their war chant. The intensity of the moment courses through Clay's veins. His entire body becomes an extension of the attack. Unleashed, he quickens. *GO! GO! GO!* His mind screams. *Let's get at 'em.* Clay's feet move faster than the drummed cadence. In a moment, the flag slaps Clay's face. He pushes through. *Get out of the way, old man,* his mind cries.

"Get back in line, you horse's ass," Dix screams. Clay retreats. A moment of light put out.

Approaching a wooded rise, the clean lines of the first steps of the advance have lost their shape as men stumble over a forest floor of fallen trees and budding bushes. Sergeant Dix and the colors are the only linear movement left, the only men able to maintain their alignment and their cadence, while the mob continues helter-skelter over branch and root. Clay fights to maintain the six paces between himself and Dix.

Breaking into a cornfield, they come upon a sea of canvas and Yankees scurrying like cockroaches caught in the light. Dix yells above the battle, "We got em,"

A pantless Yankee flies out of a tent desperately attempting to get out of harm's way, impeded only by his attempt to put a shoe on. Chaos reigns as officers and men scream orders, every man a general, every man a scared kid.

Without orders, Mississippi muskets fire into blue bodies. Sporadic fire returns. Clay reacts to the buzz that just sprinted past his head. Looking to the camp, Clay sees a Yankee in shirtsleeves methodically reloading his musket. Behind him a dozen blue bellies rally on the color line, their national colors waving frantically by the hand of a young lieutenant whose cries to "Rally" is heard by both sides. A bullet enters his throat. The colors of the United States become his funeral shroud.

Moving to the very edge of the union camp, the Confederate Army becomes an unstoppable force smashing a Wisconsin regiment in front of them. Clay looks to his company and to its first war casualty, a neighbor with a bullet through his left eye. Clay watches Alex wipe off the gore. West Pointer dies next. Without pomp or fanfare, he drops to the ground, never to see the Hudson River.

With each step another falls. With each step another kills. Clay's position makes him a spectator, so he watches Alex boiling in hatred for a Yankee he's never met. Emotions run like a raw nerve in everyone except Clay. He remains unmoved by the death of someone he went to school with or stands next to. Even the gore is impersonal, just red meat. He is dispassionate in a time of passion, and he wonders why. He has no idea why.

The colonel rides down the line desperate to regain control of his regiment. "BATTALION HALT!" Brandishing his sword in spasmodic fury, he cries out, "Halt for shit's sake!" The colors return to the ranks. The regiment finally stops.

"Dress your line, boys!" the colonel orders

Clay watches company sergeants return their charges back to the oneness of the regiment, two ranks of men again stand thirteen inches between ranks.

"Battalion Ready!" the colonel shouts as he moves to the rear of his boys.

Color Sergeant Dix continues waving the flag in broad figure eights. Muskets go to the ready, hammers go to full cock, and bodies lean in. Clay raises his musket. Intuition tells him to join the community of soldiers about to fire.

"We don't fire," Dix sounds more helpful than scorning this time. "We only fire if the colors are in danger."

Two warring ideals battle within Clay: to follow orders and not fire, or to do what his intuition says is the right thing to do. He does as he is told. His musket goes back to the shoulder.

"AIM!"

"Mississippi will be heard today," Dix beams.

"FIRE!"

Hundreds of muskets release their fury in one solid sheet of flame. Shoulders kick back as rifle butts counteract the projectiles departure. Dumbstruck, excited, and curious, the men are blinded by the smoke of battle. Clay finds his mind fixated on the waving of the flag as it moves in calm rhythm above the mayhem surrounding it. The movement reminds Clay of the swing of Uncle Frank's axe, and in that, the world becomes beautiful.

"LOAD!" the stentorian order brings Clay back to the real world.

Muskets drop and the reloading begins. Fingers dig under the leather flaps of the cartridge boxes for the paper cartridge; then bringing the round to teeth, men hungrily tear the paper tail off to expose the gunpowder. Mouths spit out the paper tail; then shaking hands push bullets and paper down musket barrels. Quickly, ramrods, awkwardly drawn, swing about, then dive down barrels. Returning ramrods, deft swings bring muskets from the ground to under right armpits. Small brass caps, mercury filled, prime the muskets. Loaded, the regiment prepares to fire again. The smoke of the previous volley has dissipated slightly. A ragged response from the Yankee lines fells three more Mississippians.

"FIRE!" Mississippi bites back. Again smoke hides the result. "Battalion, Forward…"

The colors advance again with Sergeant Dix disappearing into the smoke. Clay steps up to his position.

"March!"

The regiment again stepping as one marvels Clay. He wonders what creates such symmetry. Did those hour-upon-hour of drills cause the precision Clay sees, or is it the interconnectedness of that Oversoul? Their movement stops the philosophical questions as they enter the smoke, and the uncertainty of what lay on the other side. Will there be thousands of Yankees waiting with leveled muskets ready to kill everyone? Will there be millions? Or, will they find a harvest of the dead, sowed by smoothbore muskets and Southern mettle? The answer lies less than thirty yards away. Breaking out of the smoke, they discover an empty camp of canvas, campfires, and a dozen dead or writhing bodies. The rest have run off.

Men who have not had a proper meal in three days see a land of plenty: boxes of hard bread, slabs of bacon, and mounds of coffee lie next to bullet ridden bodies. Frying pans sizzle with half cooked bacon and coffee boils in pots while fresh bread lies half sliced. Hunger replaces duty as scores of men break ranks. Clay watches confederates who have not seen rations since Corinth leave the ranks to gorge themselves on the riches of the northern camp. Officer's too. A hunger pain reminds Clay of his last meal—yesterday. He wishes he could have gotten those sausages from the Duster Man. He begins to move toward a campfire when he hears an order.

"Stand your post, private. We have not been relieved," Dix says, standing erect. Eight men stand at attention while hundreds plunder.

Coffee pots drain steaming contents into starving mouths. A confederate captain comes out of a tent carrying a silver service set. Good tin canteens become confederate property. Nice tarred haversacks replace poorly made cotton ones. A blue regimental flag sprints to the color guard, carried by Tucker Current. "Devil to the 18th Wisconsin," he yells mockingly.

Turning to his charges, Dix explains, "Boys, we don't go in for that sort of thing until released by an officer."

Off to the right, the 15th Michigan Infantry counter attacks.

"We're up for it now, boys," yelps Tucker as he drops his trophy. He retreats. Fear begins to take over confederate soldiers as they realize the central power of the blue mass that fills their front. The glint of their bayonet prods a retrograde movement of all but the color guard. Officers desperately try to reform their companies. The colonel interposes himself between the rear and his men, "Boys, turnabout. Look there. See the color guard standing tall. Join them."

Dix waves the flag above the chaos.

"Turnabout and let's kill us a chance of Yankees!" the colonel bellows.

The force of one man's intent, as if a central voice, harkens most of the men back to where they are strongest—as one. The colonel senses the change and takes full advantage.

"On my order. Battalion Ready." Individuals become one again. "AIM!" Muskets to cheeks.

"FIRE!" a volley tears into the men from Michigan. Unfortunately for them, the bayonet is their only weapon. They were sent into battle without ammunition. They retire the bloodied fools they were sent to be.

Danger resolved for the moment, men return to their pillaging. Riding up to the color guard, the colonel sees a fellow old soldier in Sergeant Dix.

He offers a flask, "Close call there, sergeant."

Dix nods in agreement as he takes a swig. Turning to the color guard, the colonel thanks them for standing tall. "Your example stiffened this regiment." A man by a fire cries out at the pain borne from molten hot coffee. The colonel laughs, "Well, at least for a moment anyhow. Sergeant, I'm sorry I cannot relieve you to enjoy the feast, but I need the regiment to dress on you." Taking a swig, the colonel snaps a salute as he rides to the far left where he begins getting his regiment in order.

From the chaos, loaded with loot, Alex comes up to Clay.

"To the victors go the spoils," Alex points to the rest of Highland enjoying the orgy of food and supplies. "Clay, what the hell? Why don't you jump in and get you some before it's all gone," Alex demonstrates his booty like a hunter with a full bag of game.

Clay sees Alex's new haversack, a marked improvement of his linen bag already made stained beyond decency with grease, dirt, and grime. Clay also sees Alex has a new Yankee tin canteen, a much stronger vessel than Clay's leaky wood canteen. Clay can smell the bacon on Alex's breath. He begins to waver as his eyes take in a full frying pan lying on the ground just a few feet away. Just as he's about to leave the ranks, Hiram comes up carrying a tin cup.

"Thought you might like some coffee?"

Clay ends the conversation before his stomach pushes him to the cup, "I gotta stand my post." Yankee bullets begin to find the red banner above Clay's head.

"You men, move away and get back to your company," Dix orders.

Alex, in a farcical salute, moves behind Dix. Standing by Clay, he hands him a fork laden with a chunk of sizzling bacon. Like a kid sneaking the last cookie, Clay whips the bacon off the fork and into his mouth, only to discover— it's hot! He hides the pain from Dix. Wanting to spit the bacon out, he won't throw food away so instead he breaths open mouthed hoping to cool the bacon before it burns his tongue more. Fortunately, Hiram reads Clay's pain and hands him the cup of coffee.

Taking a deep drink, Clay nods a silent thank you. A bullet whizzes nearby causing the color guard to flinch.

"Man can rise above the animalist impulses and move from the rational to a spiritual realm," Hiram satirizes Emerson, Alex chews on bacon, and Clay smiles.

"You there," booms an older voice working to be heard above the growing noise of a stiffening opponent. "What's the meaning of this, lieutenant? None of that, sir."

General Albert Sidney Johnston, commander of the Confederate Army addresses a lieutenant with an armload Yankee goods. One man caught is all men caught. Hiram and Alex disappear back into the ranks. Clay quickly drops the tin cup.

"We are not here for plunder!" the general charges to all those around him. Angry that his army would do such a thing, he fumes at the lack of discipline. He pauses to refuel his tirade, when he looks at the faces of the Mississippians surrounding him. Clay sees the eyes of a general caught between the unquestioned obedience of the old army and the independent Southern men who do not take kindly to tongue lashings. The general changes his tactics. He turns to the color guard.

Seeing the tin cup next to Clay's feet, General Johnson orders, "Son, fetch that cup for me."

Clay sheepishly retrieves the cup Hiram gave him, then hands it up the general. The general raises the cup on high, announcing, "Let this be my share of the spoils today."

Instantly Johnston wins the hearts of his civilian army. Mississippi cheers. Clay loudest of all. Yankee musketry responds.

"Reform your ranks, men. Let us go after them with the same courage and determination you showed earlier. Now form up, for God's sake, and let us finish this," the general commands.

The increase of Yankee bullets adds speed to the movement of assembling men. That magnificent general waves Clay's tin cup like a marshal's baton. Clay begins to feel his place in the universe when an explosion of pain fills Clay's face. He falls.

February 1850

Sparks fly as Frank puts a fine edge to the blade of his ax when he feels the presence of someone behind him. Turning, he sees the red-faced tears of a boy who's been hit hard and often.

Frank puts down the ax then brings the boy to him.

"Uncle Frank, why?"

A black eye begins to form.

Chapter Five

October 9th, 1862

The rhythmic clack of a train's metallic wheels on iron track fills the passenger car full of the repaired pieces of the Confederate Army. From hospitals all through the Deep South, men who have suffered through camp fever, flux, or battle damage ride to Chattanooga, Tennessee, where convalescent camps dot the hills around the city. From these camps, soldiers will wait to rejoin their units.

Directly across from Clay sits two Pelicans from Louisiana, each clucking in Bayou French. Clay listens for something he recognizes as they are a study, neither one listening, both talking. *Must be a French thing,* Clay thinks, trying to understand. Surrounding him are city-bred from Nashville and Montgomery sitting next to hardscrabble farmers from the played-out regions of Georgia and North Carolina, as well as the elite from Charleston and Helena. Clay sits quietly allowing the rhythm of the rail to waft over him. Almost hypnotic, its metronomic sound reminds him of his time in Pensacola.

At first, Clay found himself drowning in army life. The never-ending noise and commotion of future soldiers was too much for him. He was an only child amongst thousands and the nonstop assault on his senses had him wanting to quit. His body hurt from the hours of drill. His mind hurt from learning how to soldier. His soul hurt from a world too intense for him. Desperate to escape, one night he took a walk on the ocean beach that formed the southern border of the camp. Once outside of camp, he passed fewer and fewer soldiers until the quiet of the ocean waves replaced the shrill sounds of his life. Immediately his mind caught the rhythm of the waves against the beach. He continued walking until he was the only one. Turning to the ocean, he watched the horizontal waves moves toward him. He watched as they lapped onto the sand then retreated. Then another. Then another. Perfect. His mind calmed.

Taking off his boots, he put his aching feet into the warm water. How delicious it felt. How healing this moment. He remembered the story of Prometheus and how the cooling winds of the ocean healed his wounds each evening. Clay looked to the west and the setting sun then to the darkness of the eastern sky. Like Prometheus, the vultures will again chew at Clay in the morning. Like Prometheus, Clay has the evening to heal so every night he wasn't on duty, he would come to this spot to heal. Some evenings he would sit on the shore watching the porpoises glide through the waves. How peaceful and graceful they were as they slid out of sight then crested in graceful perfection.

The train hit several bumps.

One night as Clay watched dolphins playing, he heard the yipping sounds of soldiers coming up the beach. A musket's crack followed by cheering when a dolphin frothed red, peace was destroyed that night and worse the next night when Alex and Tucker came to the beach, muskets in hand. Clay watched as Tucker took careful aim. Tucker didn't miss. Reloading his musket, he offered it to Clay.

"Yea, Clay, take a shot," Alex chimed in.

In a moment that disgusted Clay, he did as he was told.

"Aim just ahead of him," Tucker instructed.

Clay aimed for the tail and fired

"Can't believe you missed. Did ya lead em?" Tucker groaned.

Alex knew the answer.

The train rattles at an uneven rail. Next to Clay the sleeping Irishman drops ass then smiles at the dryness of his product. Clay puts his head out the window to escape the spewing gas suitable for a cannon's mouth, or an Irishman's ass. Breathing deep, Clay enjoys the crispness of the air and the peace found in the passing red leaves of the oak and whiteness of the birch. A fox retreats behind a rock, its supper limply hanging from its mouth. In nature beauty lives alongside ugly.

The train begins an ascent up one of the steep ridges that surrounds Chattanooga, the change in angle pushing coal exhaust past Clay's window, forcing him to retreat back into the car.

"What a stink," Clay's bench mate belches. "Close the damnable window, would ya!"

Clay closes the window just as the train peaks the ridge. He gets his first view of Chattanooga. A former frontier town, the construction of the Memphis and Charleston rail line, as well as the river, turned it into an 1850's boom town of two thousand people. It's nestled in a deep valley surrounded by ridges on three sides and a river on the other. The strategic value of the river and railroad has made Chattanooga a significant artery of the Confederacy. Clay feels the train begin its descent into the valley.

The train tilts downhill, the rhythmic clanking growing closer and closer till it becomes one metallic sound. The belching smoke becomes a thin ribbon in the foreground of a blur of the landscape. The poorly maintained track forces the car to and fro in increasing intensity. In the minds of men not used to going faster than a horse at gallop, heart beats increase as the innate danger of a patchwork train speeding up on worn out rails. The descent sharpens. A sudden jolt shakes Clay, thrusting his mind back to the train wreck that first introduced him to mass carnage.

February 26th, 1862

Early spring 1862, a crisp dawn awakes to a train full of newly minted soldiers heading north to join General Beauregard in central Tennessee. Nine hundred Mississippians fill every nook and cranny of the train with scores forced to ride on top of the cars where the choking black smoke and coal embers torment Clay, Tucker, Alex and the rest of their company. The train sprints its twenty-five miles per hour past small towns and piney woods. Before long familiar sites pass their view. The commotion of men about to see home again grows with each landmark recognized. They pass the Current farm. Clay grows quieter. At the edge of Highland, the train whistle blows. The boys hoot and holler as they see the spire of First Baptist. The train slows to a stop in front of the station and is immediately engulfed by a throng of mothers, fathers, sweethearts, and siblings all searching for relatives gone for too long.

"Hey, Clay, lookie, there they is," Alex cries out pointing to his family.

The train barely stops when Alex and the rest of the company leap off and into waiting arms. The Current boys receive a basket of food from their mother. Will Rutledge, a neighbor of Clay's, is awash in his four children. Husbands hug wives and mothers hold their own close one more time.

Looking in the direction of Lick Creek, Clay listens for the sound of the axe he knows he can't hear. He thinks of Frank swinging his axe. He then imagines his mother, her sad countenance hidden in a cup of coffee and a vacant stare out the window. He misses her. A quick movement catches his attention. Below him George Stewart slices through the crowd calling for his wife Julie. A jailed emotion escapes in a suppressed cry as Clay too searches for her in a sea of multi-colored dresses. George's yell, "Julie!" has Clay following his voice to her. She kisses George deeply. Clay turns away. While the train refuels and families reunite, Clay looks over the crowd to a patch of woods beyond the town where the sun begins its downward movement Fortunately for Clay, the urgencies of war has the train needed north so the stop is brief. In short order the train slowly pulls away from Highland.

That same night a freight train carrying logs heading south is on the same track as Clay's northbound train. Two hours north of Highland, the two trains collide. The engine and the first two cars splinter into a mass of wood, crushed steel, and twenty-two mangled bodies. Sixteen more cry out in agony. The boys from Highland are on the fifth car in line. They are safe except for having to help clear the carnage. Clay put a severed arm in a bag.

The downward movement of the train has the Irishman swearing at Clay like it's his fault.

"Gorach pios cac" (stupid piece of shit).

The train sways side to side, each sway a little more than the last. One long sway to the right ends in a hard smack back on both rails. Some of the passengers laugh and yelp in freakish play while others hang on for dear life.

"Mhac na galla," (son of a bitch), his pendulum eyes search for an end.

The train gains speed. Clay's heart sprints. A world barely understood brings a tear to his mind. It's not the fear of death that fills Clay. It's the fear of not living that chokes him.

The train sways high on one set of wheels then lands

in another jolt, but softer than the last one. The downward angle of Clay's seat softens. The whirr is replaced by a clack as the Chattanooga Valley welcomes them. The Irishman crawls back into his shoulders as that laughter brought from fear unrealized fills the car. Still alive.

"Pog mo thoin," (kiss my ass) The Irishman gives Clay one last look.

The train crosses Chestnut Street then slows to a stop in front of Union Station. Climbing into the car, a sergeant fills the aisle. "Clear the train and fall in on the platform,"

Stepping onto the platform, Clay sees mountains of ammunition, new cannons freshly forged in a Richmond mill, and rations in the form of barrels of salt pork and sacks of cornmeal. He has returned to the bayonet point of war.

"Fall in for roll call," the sergeant orders.

Twenty-five men shuffle to form up. Behind Clay, the Frenchmen continue their diatribe. One, older and more grizzled than his comrade, looks to the sergeant, "sucer mon âne?" They giggle to each other like schoolgirls. The sergeant shakes his head then turns to the roster given to him by the conductor. Seeing the ragged condition of the line, he becomes even more sergeant like.

"By height, two ranks."

Clay begins to find his place when the sergeant sees him. "You there. The tall one."

Clay responds like he does to any authoritarian voice. He freezes.

"You're acting corporal. Stand here," the sergeant points to a spot on the mud splattered deck.

Clay becomes a corporal. His mind tastes something new. He begins to smile. He begins to feel important. He begins to stand a bit taller.

"Just stand there."

Clay shrinks.

"Fall in, boys, so we can get you to the convalescent camp then back to your regiments." The sergeant continues, "Attention Company. Right Dress." Bodies immediately straighten up, touching elbow to elbow as each head turns slightly to the right. A man with a bandaged neck groans, the movement tearing at his scab.

"Front." They straighten as much as their injuries will allow. The man with the neck wound winces as he turns his head.

With that the sergeant turns to his right to salute a collection of officers. The ranking officer, a captain, receives and returns the sergeant's salute then steps toward them; the captain's glare freezes Clay.

"I'm Captain Hightower. While the army is in Kentucky, you will be in my charge."

"Sergeant, take the formation to camp."

"Yes, Sir. Company Right, Face." Pivoting on worn heals, the formation follows orders. "Forward, march."

Shoes on dirt road make tracks. Wagons on a muddy road makes ruts. Thousands of shoes and wagons on a country road make a quagmire of shoe-sucking mud.

One man swears as he feels the mud slime over the top of his shoe. In a comical and grotesque movement, each man moves like he's pulling taffy with his feet. Sometimes the shoe stays with the foot and other times the remnant of a grimy sock stands divorced from a shoe still half submerged.

"Mhac na galla," The Irishman belches, his shoe still in the mud.

And so they move down the road filled with wagons driven by the vilest men on earth—teamsters. Since Clay was a boy he's known teamsters intimately. Shit on in life and so they return the favor to anyone crossing their path. Mr. Miller did some teamster work, bringing the mindset home to his family. A wagon approaches Clay.

"Move aside there, yous sons a bitches, er I'll run yer ass over to make better footin' for these beasts." Spittle spews from the teamster's mouth and stains his chin. His wagon passes a chorus of verbal threats given by the column of soldiers, except Clay.

A half mile out and already the weak pollute the roadside. The grizzled Pelican falls out where he lays on the bank rubbing his knee and yelling to his pard in their tongue. The younger one moves on, appearing glad to be free. The sergeant turns to the old Frenchmen, "Adieu, mon ami," and continues.

Seeing a friend leave a friend reminds Clay of his leaving Hiram alone with Alex and the rest of Highland. Guilty not for choosing Alex over Hiram back in Corinth and not being able to apologize before Shiloh, he wonders if Hiram is glad to be rid of him. His mind wrestles with what he should have done: accept both parts of his life instead of thinking he had to choose.

"Two more miles and we'll be there," the sergeant tells the men. Three more fall out. "We'll send a wagon for these here," words that send two more to the roadside. The sergeant shakes his head, "Coffee coolers."

Clay, having never heard the term before, he grows curious, "Sergeant, what's a coffee cooler?"

The sergeant responds, "They make coffee while real men do their duty. They quit when things get tough. They run away from battle." He puts his hand on Clay's shoulder. "Slackers. Men without value. What not to be."

Rounding a wooded bend, the column crosses a lazy stream, its banks festooned with men filling canteen or emptying themselves in the only water source for the nearly six hundred soldiers waiting for General Braxton Bragg's and General Kirby Smith's southern armies to return. The grapevine has brought news that Bragg is about to pitch into the federals somewhere in Northern Kentucky. Somewhere up there Alex and Hiram are tasting gunpowder. Feeling guilty for being away since April, the omnipresent pain in his cheek reminds Clay of his time since Shiloh.

On a once-profitable farm, the army has set up a convalescent camp among its buildings and on its once-grand front yard. At the entrance to the camp an evergreen arbor announces the name—Camp Hightower. The arbor proves a presumptuous entrance for a camp of dirty canvas tents and rough soldier shanties. The white washed clapboards of the big house have long been turned into siding for soldier's cabins. Crossing the front lawn, now the parade ground, the moving column becomes an oracle for the hundreds of men searching for comrades or news.

"Hey, anyone here from the 5th Kentucky?" a camp soldier barks into the column

"Looking for the 1st Arkansas." Eyes search for comrades.

"Texas?"

Clay hears a familiar voice calling his name, a voice he never thought he would hear outside of Highland.

"Mista Clay."

February 1850

Clay follows Frank into the woodlot where he sits on a stump pouting because he can't do what a man can do. Pinging a hatchet against branches is all he can do with his boy's strength. He wants to be strong. He wants to make wood chips explode off a trunk. He wants to knock down a tree with an axe just like Frank. More than that, he wants something else. Regardless of how hot or how cold, how late in the day, or how tired Frank is, the sable face of the Mr. Miller's slave glows inner peace. Frank hands his favorite ax, Old Thunder, to Clay.

"Take Old Thunda and give it a crack, boy," Frank parents.

Clay sees him. Frank! His feet begin to follow his eyes when a horse blocks his way. Looking up, Clay sees Captain Hightower glaring at him. Clay retreats and the captain rides on.

"Attention, Company," barks the sergeant. Men struggle to find the step. Coming abreast of some large tents and the flagpole, he commands, "HALT. Front. Right Dress." The column does as its told. "Front." The formation faces the officer. "Sir, the company is formed," the sergeant offers a warm salute.

Captain Hightower returns the note of respect then turns to the formation of men before him. Dismounting, he stands right in front of Clay; then, smelling the air, he adjusts his kepi in foul disgust. Clay's eyes fall to the ground.

"Do not shat anywhere you please. This is not your mother's parlor. Use the sinks. Make water there too." Each group that arrives to camp gets the same lecture. "Billet where you can for now, and mind your behavior, for I will not stand any shenanigans."

He points to an oak tree where two men hang by their thumbs—their outstretched hands reaching up as if trying to pluck fall leaves from the branches to which they hang. The taller of the two has been given the sterner sentence, for he sways like a flag in the breeze, tied up so his toes barely touch the very top of the grass. The shorter one has a good grasp of the ground, so he pushes toes into earth to take the pressure from his swollen thumbs.

Hightower turns back toward Clay, "Those two men didn't show respect for the rules of this camp and this army. Is that clear?"

The formation is dismissed and just as quickly Clay's mind returns to Frank. His eyes swim through the mass of white faces for Frank while his mind remembers the last time he saw Frank, that day in the sorghum field.

October 1861

Behind Clay lies rumpled bedding while in front of him awaits the uniform of a confederate soldier. Since he returned from college, he's worked the fields. He'd done something else. He enlisted. Putting on his blue shirt with red cuffs and collar, he moves about as quietly as possible. Clay slides down to his shoes; made of leather, they have carried him from farm to college, from college to farm. Now they'll get him away. Moving downstairs, he arrives to a stone-cold stove and last night's biscuits—his farewell meal. Putting them in his pocket, he leaves for the barn where he hid his musket and military furniture the night before. Nearing the barn, he hears the sound of the sharpening wheel. Entering the barn, he sees his military furniture laying at Frank's feet, the old smoothbore polished to a fine sheen. The leathers have been oiled as well. He also sees Frank's axe on the ground, and curious what Frank's sharpening, Clay moves to see his bayonet sparking. Frank feels the boy's arrival.

"Ya can cut meat with this thing now," he turns to Clay. "Be careful, boy." Clay watches him go somewhere in thought then shake himself back to the present. "Livin at bayonet point has done men in."

Not sure what Frank means, and in a hurry to leave before Mr. Miller stops him, Clay says goodbye, "I'm leavin now, Uncle Frank." In Clay's eagerness to escape the Miller farm, it isn't until this moment he realizes he's leaving Frank as well.

"To gets away?"

Clay knows what Frank's asking. Clay is not joining to fight for slavery. "No other reason, I promise." Clay lies to himself, "I'll be back by hog killin."

Standing up, Frank offers a handshake. "Then you best be goin. Massa Miller be a early risa." He hands Clay his musket and gear. "Take care, boy."

"I will."

And Clay Miller moves down the Miller farm lane to town where he will board a train to anywhere but here.

While recovering from his Shiloh wound, Clay had a chance to return home and the idea of seeing Frank again almost urged him to.

"Clay!"

Black and white meet.

"Hey, look at that boy huggin that nigga like he's Pappy hisself," a voice condemns.

Removing himself, Frank gets his first look at Clay.

"You looking a bit worn, Mista Clay. Olda even." Tilting his head to inspect the right side of Clay's face,

Frank notices the jagged, reddened line running from cheek to mouth.

Clay explains, "Where the bullet went in. And where the surgeons dug it out."

A bit of yellow puss seeps out from the upper edge of the wound. In a well-practiced move Clay gently wipes it away.

"The doctor said puss means healing," Clay explains.

"See if we can get you well, Mista Clay." With that Frank takes Clay by the arm and heads him out of the crowd and toward the camp area. "Some boys from near home is stayin' under da shed. Yer cousin Dave Porta is ones of em. He and a dull-witted boy from Milford."

He leads Clay to a three-sided shebang made from farmhouse siding and canvas. By comparison with the gopher holes and lean-tos filling the field, this structure stands firm and resolute. Inside the shebang Dave Porter, Clay's cousin on his mother's side, sews a button on an oft-mended shirt. Next to him sits a squirrelish boy from Milford sitting open mouthed, watching Dave sew. Dave, city bred and illiterate in the ways of a saw or hammer, and Milford's fascination with the magic of sewing leaves only one possible builder of the shebang.

"Frank, you built this?"

"I did," Frank offers with pride. Skill trumps color when white men are in need, so Dave and Milford treat Frank decently.

Cousin Dave, the wag of his mother's family, and

continuing the art of sarcasm even in the army, offers his first salvo. "Clay, the two-faced boy: black and blue on the side and whitewashed as a whore on her wedding night on the other." He pauses in exaggerated inspection of the difference between the two sides of Clay's face. "I always felt Old Man Miller hankered darker meat, but I never guessed you were the spawn of his dalliance."

A firm punch in the chest, delivered with a smile, leaves Dave fighting for a breath and Clay catches himself surprised at where that instinctive movement came from. Milford, dull eyed and open mouthed, chortles. He offers Clay his name and just as quick, it's lost. Forever on he will be Milford. Frank stands where he's supposed to—in the back—a proud smile on his face.

"How you been doin?" Frank's genuine voice asks.

Like a kid coming home from an eventful day of school, Clay tells wide-eyed stories of his time in the color guard, Shiloh, the hospital, and his promotion to corporal, given just today. Frank listens intently to every word, responding in the way only a true listener can. Even Dave and Milford listen for a bit. Suddenly the realization of Frank in a Chattanooga convalescence camp hits Clay.

"How did you get here?"

Frank explains, "Kept fallin, fallin behind wit my work. Massa Miller had me cuttn' wood an workn' the farm. It plain wore me out, so one day I'z fell sleep out by Lick Creek. He founds me. Massa Miller scolded me fierce then cuz' I kept up my lazy nigger ways.' He hired Bab McNally right out.

Then he told my lazy self to get somewheres useful. Gave me my papers he did. Ima gessin he figured it be cheaper if I died a free man than he hads bury me a slave. Even stopped feedin' me. So I comes here. Hopes ya don't mind?"

Clay sees that Mr. Miller was right in evaluating Frank's monetary value, Frank's one stooped shoulders and bent back would fetch very little on the slave market.

"You sure are a sight for sore eyes, Uncle Frank."

For the next few hours Clay tells Frank about life in the army. When Clay asks about home, Frank protects the boy by talking about crops and neighbor gossip. "You's mama is doing tolerable," is all he says about the Miller home. Without recognizing it, it's all Clay really wants to know about home. Eventually exhaustion provides an escape from thinking about home as Clay's eyes grow heavy and his responses to conversation becomes slurred and unimaginative. Since the Shiloh wound, it's always the same; in the morning he feels strong, but as the day wears on, regardless of the amount of work he does, a heavy feeling fills his head. The doctors said it's the healing process, and it will pass.

"Might be times to turn in, Mista Clay. Where's your truck?" Frank leads Clay closer to the shelter.

"I am a man without property, Uncle Frank," Clay explains his condition. "The hospital provided a new uniform, a cup, and spoon." Clay looks to his worn work shoes made worse by the miles.

"Mista Clay, yous can haz my blankets ifn you wants?"

Handing Clay his blanket, Frank turns to go, "Best get some firewood in fer the cold gets a hold of us. Night be nigh on comin."

"Get enough for breakfast tomorrow," Dave orders as he gets ready for bed.

Milford establishes himself next to Dave. "You got a good darkie there, Clay."

"Clay, tuck between us. Keep warm that way," the cousin offers.

Meanwhile Frank's pulls something from the shebang. Clay watches as the long black oak handle comes out from the blanket then the well sharpened head of Ole Thunder. Clay smiles as the two best parts of his youth shine before him. Putting the axe to shoulder, Frank begins moving away when the idea of joining Frank in the woods again, of seeing his axe swing again, invigorates Clay.

"Wait up. I'll give a hand." Clay says, moving toward Frank, "Mind?"

Frank hands Clay the axe and they walk side by side in the silence of two people with a deep history.

Coming to the woodlot, Clay hands Frank his axe, wishing he had one too.

"No sa. You gets first swing." Looking around, Frank picks out an anemic looking pine. "The branches be crunchy."

Clay snaps, "That twig." Insulted, he moves to a slightly stouter birch. When Clay was young, the heavy blade and long handle proved too much for his skinny frame. It wasn't until just a year before college that he proved strong enough to make a serious impression on a tree. He takes a swing. Today Old Thunder feels as heavy as when he was a kid as the blade slaps at the birch then tips to the ground. His muscles are weak. Even his bones are tired. Clay returns the axe to Frank. "Sorry." Clay wipes off a bead of pus from his wound.

"No worries, Mista Clay. Let's see ifn ole Frank cans knock this stubborn fella down."

Frank make his first swing. Wood chips fly. Another swing and the same result, yet Clay isn't seeing the same Frank. As a younger man, Frank used his axe blade like a maul and his muscle like the sledgehammer. As Clay grew stronger, he used brute force to drive tree to ground. Now, stooped shouldered and worn down, Frank has adapted his swing by employing a slight twist just before the blade hits.

Turning to Clay, Frank explains, "Too old to grunt the ole tree down. Neva could quit so I hadsa finds me a new way. This old head just thought of it."

"Let me take a stab at it, Frank." Wood chips fly. The mind trumps muscle.

October 10th, 1862

A landscape frosted white greets the predawn glow to drum sticks striking the rhythmic cadence of 'wake-up' and a pair of fifes offering their whimsical notes to another day in Camp Hightower. Dave is the first one out from his blankets, when he sees something alarming.

"Oh, my word," Dave's words awaken Clay. Through his left eye Clay sees Dave's ashen face staring at him. "You need to see the doctor," Dave offers in a voice of concern and disgust. "I can barely see where your eye goes."

Blind in one eye, scared in the other, Clay cries for help, but fears the source of that help. The alarm in Dave's voice has Clay imagining the worst. Struggling to see, Clay feels a nauseating dizziness threaten to drop him.

"Your face is pissin," Dave declares.

Clay touches his cheek, and in doing so the wound opens up, puss dribbling down his face. He begins to give in when a firm hand holds him up.

"Don't quit, boy."

Walking alone, one-eyed and dizzy, Clay moves past wagons unloading men and goods, past hospital stewards with stained forearms, and past closed tents of pain. To the left, he sees a tent with an open flap. Clay enters only to slam into the biggest black man he's ever seen. Clay begins to blackout.

"Sorry, suh," says the man. Clay feels a powerful arm hold him up as if he were a child. "I didn't see ya there, massa."

A white orderly arrives and knowing exactly what to do, brings Clay into a tent that assaults his senses with rotting flesh, dysentery, and urine, a smelling salt that ignites his faculties. Looking around, he sees woolen blankets outlining missing limbs and hollowed-eyed souls fighting for one more breath. Revolted and afraid he'll be

one of them, Clay attempts to leave when a vice-like grip
stops his movement.

"Where are you going?" It's Captain Hightower.

"Tent's full. I'll come back later," Clay struggles with
the stabbing pain.

Taking a long look at his new patient, Hightower
orders, "You'll do no such thing. Orderly, take this man to
the surgical chair."

Oh shit. Clay feels himself being manhandled by the
white orderly's firm hold on his elbow and wrist. Taking
him toward the back of the tent, they pass cot after cot
of pitying eyes and knowing nods. Each nod intensifies
Clay's growing fear. Clay learned after Shiloh that doctors
are not gentle when inspecting wounds.

They move behind a canvas partition that separates the
patients from the surgical area. Clay's good eye struggles
to clarify his surroundings. The first thing he sees is a door
laid out over two barrels, its once green paint stained with
the blood of the captain's handy work. Next to it sits an
oaken chair with leather straps attached to each arm and
the front legs. The deeply grooved sod just in front of the
chair shows the struggles of those who have sat there
before.

"Sit there," the orderly commands in a voice that leaves
no room for discussion. Clay meekly falls into the chair.
Helpless, he watches the doctor methodically clean his
glasses then, looking at his patient, a slight smile comes
across the doctor's face.

"What's your name, soldier?" Hightower lowers himself in order to begin his investigation. The professional courtesy makes Clay feel a bit better.

"Clay Miller."

"I'm Doctor Hightower, Private Miller. You've got one fine infection there. Good thing you came in today. I'll be as gentle as possible, but there is something inside your wound that is causing this infection. A piece of bone maybe, or a piece of bullet. If we don't get it out, you won't see Sunday. Brace yourself. The journey to full health is a long one."

Clay's good eye opens wide. *What does he mean?* Hightower's gentle touch sends a shot of pain through his patient. Clay explodes like an animal beat one too many times. The doctor flies across the room. White hot spasms of pain shoot from Clay's face through his entire body. He feels bile rising up his throat. His body wants to run away. His mind wants to quit the pain. Looking over, he sees Hightower crawl to where his glasses landed. Clay, like a wounded animal waiting for the final attack, watches the doctor silently clean the grass from the lenses.

Moving to check on the doctor, the orderly looks back to Clay, "Boy, you sure fixed yaself on that one. Doc don't take kindly to disrespect." Clay well knows the punishment for disrespecting his 'betters.'

"Fetch Leon," Hightower tells the orderly.

"Yes, Sir."

Brushing grass off his sleeves, Hightower walks over to

his medical bag. The sound of metal instruments clanging tells of a search for the right instrument. Hightower pulls a scalpel, its smallish blade would be laughable in a river town bar fight, but here it menaces like a Bowie Knife. Hightower inspects the blade closely then looks to Clay.

Reeling from the pain of Hightower's initial probe, Clay still finds himself proud of his protective reaction feeling a bit like the night he shoved Mr. Miller from off his mother. Once, when he was helping Frank, a log jammed his finger. Tears welled up and all he wanted to do was run home, when Frank grabbed him. Clay fought like a trapped animal the whole time, but was helpless to stop the more powerful man. Frank righted the finger. Glad to see the fight still in the boy, Frank offered fatherly advice, "Never quit."

The orderly reenters with Leon, whose powerful build and massive hands move in. With strength equal to the challenge, Leon begins with Clay's arms. Grabbing a wrist Leon forces it to the arm of the chair while Clay squirms to free it. Clay fights to break the iron grip as Leon works firmly but gently to hold the wrist against the arm of the chair. The white orderly straps Clay's wrist down. The next wrist falls easier. Exhausted, but still fighting, Clay tries to protect his legs.

"It will hurt worse if you fight," Hightower says standing in front of Clay. The shining scalpel and stained leather apron mock the boy from Highland.

Shit! Clay wants to continue the fight yet the effect of

the probing and fighting have made him weak and before he can muster one more fight, Leon takes one of Clay's legs and slams it against the chair leg, the orderly quickly tying the strap round it. Moving to the free leg, he does the same. Finished, Leon rises, a smile that salts the wound.

Looking over Clay's head, Hightower nods, and in a moment Leon's python arm puts Clay in a headlock.

What would Frank say to the boy sitting in the chair? Shackled against his will, Clay cries inside. He wants to run. He wants to quit. He wants to stand up, but he can't. He is bound by straps stronger than he is.

"Clay," Hightower's voice filters in. "I need to clean your wound. Please don't fight us. We're here to help."

Help? A word not heard during any beating he ever had before.

"Leon, tight but not too tight."

Clay feels the smothering firmness of the grip around his forehead tighten, yet not hurting. Leon has taken away Clay's ability to fight, yet in practiced placement, he protects Clay.

"There, Mista. Be calm. Take whaz good fer ya," he whispers in Clay's left ear.

"Ready, Leon?"

"Yessa."

Hightower looks directly into the good eye, "I'm about to make an incision just below your right eye." He draws closer. "I need to drain the wound before I can find out what's causing the infection. You've fought this infection alone for quite some time, but you need our help before it's too late."

"Sir, should I administer ether?" the orderly inquires.

"No."

A line of intense fire slows time as the blade burns its way across Clay's cheek. Hot liquid flows. Clay passes out.

October 12th, 1862

"Private Miller. Good to see you in the land of the living," the gentle voice of Hightower awakens Clay. "We thought we lost you."

Clay's left eye looks into the compassionate eyes of the doctor. He watches as Hightower gently unwraps the bandage covering the wound. Pulling up a puss soaked pad of cotton, he inspects it carefully. Smiling, he hands it to an equally smiling Leon.

"Well, it looks like you've turned the corner. Good thing you didn't quit."

The doctor sees the question in Clay's eye.

"You had a severe infection." He puts on a clean bandage and rewraps the wound. "The surgeons who treated you left a piece of bone floating about. That's where the infection came from."

"Did you get it out?"

"Yes," he says, proud of his craft. You'll have some seeping for a couple of days. We'll change the bandages until it stops and then send you on your way." He smiles and pats Clay on the shoulder. Pivoting to Leon, Clay watches as the doctor's demeanor changes from caregiver to man in charge.

"This man will not be released until he is completely healed," Leon salutes the doctor's orders. "Change his bandage twice a day. I'll do the third." With that, the doctor moves to the next bed where a leg-less man lies in a pool of misery.

For the next few days, Clay heals. Each day Leon brings a broth of pork, Irish potatoes, onion, and plantain. Each day Clay eats more. At first the bandages scare Clay because they are full of dried red and yellowish seepage. With the passing of time, less and less infection runs out until barely a drop stains the cotton bandage.

"Well, son, you did well." Hightower finishes replacing the bandage, "A lot of these men don't have that spark of life you have. Those are the ones who don't make it."

Clay looks around at too many cots filled with too many vacant eyes.

"You have it, son."

Clay is beginning to see it too.

October 17th, 1862

Clay watches Doctor Hightower go from cot to cot offering kindness and expertise to each patient. At first Clay shied away from the compassion shown by Hightower. Clay was raised on hardness, but as he heals, he softens.

"Well, Clay, you've made fine progress. The wound is healing nicely, your color is good. According to Leon, your appetite is excellent so that means in a day or two, you'll be released." Hightower tells Clay to, "Pull your sleeve up so I can see your arm."

"Sure."

Just as Clay has his sleeve as far up as he can, the doctor takes a scalpel and makes a small cut on Clay's upper arm. The intense pain has Clay coiled and ready to strike when the soft voice of trust stops him.

"What was that for?" Clay says, watching the blood run from the incision.

"The army is returning and reports say there's smallpox in some of the Tennessee regiments. Need to protect you from smallpox."

Next, he pulls a scab between two folds of wax paper. He places the scab on the incision; then wraps a bandage around the wound. Clay struggles to continue the trust.

"What was that?"

"A scab I harvested from a smallpox patient."

Revolted by the idea of someone's scab placed on his cut, Clay's mind battles. Caught between his respect for the doctor and what the doctor just did, Clay stands in confused silence when a wave of noise floods the tent. Dave, Milford, and Frank rush to him.

"Hey, Clay," yelps Milford. "Brought ya something."

"SSSHHHHHHH," Leon warns. Milford glares at the insolence of a darky telling him what do to.

"Let em in, Leon," Dr. Hightower orders as he moves to another patient.

Dave plops down on the side of the bed to examine Clay's now barely bandaged face.

"Smaller for sure, but, not committed to it being an improvement." He sees the fresh bandage on Clay's arm. "What gives? I didn't know you was wounded on the arm too."

They all laugh as Clay gently punches Dave in the chest.

"Where you boys been? Man thinks he has comrades then dies of loneliness," Clay says. He had begun missing his companions soon after the surgery.

Dave responds quickly, "We did stop by the first night." He grows solemn. "You weren't good, Clay. The doctor told us you might not see the morning. He told us to let you rest so we stayed away till invited. The doc sent that big fella to get us. That's why we're here today."

"That's one of biggest darkies I ever did see," pipes in Milford. "Might see about buyin' him fer the farm." Clay spits at the idea of Doctor Highland selling Leon to work Milford's farm, for even owning Leon.

Dave turns to Frank, "Go ahead, Frank, show em."

From behind Frank, worn hands bring forth a sweet pumpkin pie then Milford brings out a canteen full of molasses which he over-generously pours on the pie. For the remainder of the night the boys share food and good cheer. They even share their feast with the orderly and, at Clay's insistence, Leon.

"Where did you ever get such a pie, Frank?"

"Some questions best not be answered, Mista Clay."

The next morning Clay awakes feeling better than he ever has, until the doctor walks in. Usually Hightower's inspections are adorned with kindness. Today's examination feels colder.

"Private Miller. This swelling I'm pushing on comes from healing. Before, your body was too busy fighting infection to heal the fractured bone. Now your body rebuilds the area where the bullet skipped off your cheek." He laughs at his word choice then hardens again. The captain has replaced the doctor.

"Private, you are ready for release." He then motions to the tent opening where the sergeant and two provost guards wait. "Sergeant, over here."

"Sir, is this the man?"

"Yes, sergeant." Hightower turns to Clay. "Private Miller, the military does not allow a private soldier to have familiars with officers. For bodily assault on an officer, you are to be punished."

For the next three hours Clay hangs by his thumbs, his feet resting firmly on the ground. For the remainder of Clay's time in Camp Hightower, he promptly and sincerely offers a salute to the captain's coat and a doctor's heart.

Chapter Six

October 19ᵗʰ, 1862

An army in retreat arrives like a rainstorm. First, the foreboding sky of news from the front warns everyone of what's coming; then sporadic drops begin as the early wounded, sick, and coffee coolers trickle back. Camp Hightower feels the first few drops in the form of wagon loads of slightly wounded crying out as the potholes in the road slam them into each other. Then the cloud burst of thousands of soldiers tramping back from defeat fills every space around the camp. Camp Hightower is flooding with men in urgent need of help, so Hightower acts quickly to bring in reinforcements for his effort to save men's lives.

The white orderly finds Clay near his lean-to. "Miller. Report to Captain Hightower."

"Right away," Clay responds rubbing his thumbs.

Pushing through the growing chaos, he finds the captain directing the wounded.

Hightower smiles. "I need a sergeant to gather a detail to smooth out the camp road, and you're it."

"Sergeant?" Clay balks.

Clay ponders being a sergeant for a day. *Not much of an honor*, he thinks when Hightower gives Clay his first detail. "You will fill the rank for as long as you are in my command. Too congested to start today, so begin at first light, Sergeant Miller."

In a camp of confederate soldiers, Clay walks humbly to his billet, his eyes cast to the ground while his heart fills with the idea of someone seeing merit in him. Even as a child Clay hungered for validation. From grades at school, to the size of a trout caught while fishing with Alex, he wanted Mr. Miller to say 'that-a-boy,' or words never spoken—'I'm proud of you.' Even though Alex used to tell him not worry about what folks thought. "It's a fine fish, Clay. Ain't that enough?" Clay stilled yearned to feel valued.

Coming up to the shed, he sees Milford staring at nothing while Tennessee, a new guy who joined the mess the other day, rips the black wool tape from his military pants. Frank is off with Dave to forage some food for supper.

Clay finds Tennessee's actions curious. "Hey, what ya doin?"

"This damned tape is half fallin off. Who needs this fancy military silliness anyway? Stripes don't make a man better than another."

Tennessee's words and actions reminds Clay of the distaste for authority that is so ingrained in the Southern soldier. The challenge of his new position becomes clearer.

"Why you called to the captain?" Tennessee asks.

"He made me a sergeant," Clay folds his arms across his chest.

"Saw it comin all along," Milford says matter of fact.

"What?" Clay drops his arms.

"Plain as day. Some have it, some ain't." Tennessee shares what it seems like they all feel.

Just then Frank and Dave return with armfuls of corn and sweet potatoes.

"Our Clay is now a sergeant," Milford beams.

Milford's surprising announcement sings an unfamiliar song, one Clay needs validation before he accepts it.

"Damn straight. Let's celbrate wit some corn," Frank beams pride.

Feeling awkward, Clay quickly takes the corn and begins shucking.

Milford challenges the action, "Let your nigga do that so we can celebrate your promotion with game of euchre."

Frank moves in to take the corn like society expects him to when Clay gently pushes Frank's hands away, "I got it."

Clay gives his first order while shucking corn for the mess, "I need you fellas to give a hand on a detail first thing tomorrow." Sergeant Clay passes his first test.

October 20th, 1862

Morning sees Clay frantically digging through blankets and gear for his jacket while trying not to wake up his messmates, and also finding Frank's spot empty.

Shit. He knows Hightower will not appreciate Clay leading the detail in his shirtsleeves. He feels phantom pain in his thumbs.

"What the hell are you doing, Clay?" Dave chuckles.

"Can't find my jacket. Have you seen it? Shit, where could it be?" Clay continues as his comrades slide to one side of the shelter.

"Check in Frank's truck."

Clay searches the empty blanket of Frank's bed. Nothing. *What the hell.* He continues to dig.

"Mista Clay," the sable voice calls. All eyes turn to Frank holding Clay's jacket up high. On each sleeve three black wool chevrons transform a private's jacket into a symbol of promotion.

"Looks better on your jacket than my pants," Tennessee beams. "Put it on."

Overwhelmed with gratitude, embarrassment, confusion, honor, and pride, Clay Miller gracefully accepts the gift. "Thank you," is his meiosis. Frank helps his boy.

"What are your orders?" Dave snaps to attention.

"Fall in." They do. Tennessee spits a wad of chaw.

Taking a deep breath, Clay addresses his command, "Captain Hightower wants us to smooth out the camp road." Clay's first command posture is based on what he always wanted from those who directed him, an explanation of why, "He wants us to make sure the camp road is smooth so the wounded don't suffer any more than they already are."

They've all heard the ungodly screams of the wounded men so no one can deny the logic of the order. Clay turns away and begins walking toward the supply tent when he feels a distance growing between himself and the rest. Turning back, he sees Dave, Milford, and Tennessee waiting for orders. Even Frank joins the line.

"Oh, hell," Private Miller learns a bit about being Sergeant Miller, "Detail, Right Face." Four bodies turn his way. "Forward, at the route step. March." The detail laughs as they move to Clay's step. Clay smiles.

Grabbing shovels, Clay begins to define his leadership style by working harder than the rest. Dave is not a bad worker. Neither is Milford, except for his many breaks to make water. Tennessee is flat out lazy. Only Frank works as hard, or as fast as Clay, the two creating a competition the others can't keep up with. Night comes with a job well done.

The next morning, Hightower's second order to Sergeant Miller is to burn the uniforms of the wounded before their putrescent infects the camp. Hightower doesn't want disease spreading. On the fifth day, Clay buries a piles of limbs while the others bury fifteen bodies that Hightower couldn't save. On the sixth day, so many sick and wounded have arrived that Clay and his mates lose their shed to them. They now call the ground under the 'thumb oak' their home. On the eighth day, while the rest of the detail works on the road again, Clay becomes a hospital steward, in charge of a tent full of men recovering from amputation. He replaces bandages, removes the dead, and renders the wounded what succor he can.

A week later the full flood of the army arrives in the form of tens of thousands of weary troops and thousands of emaciated horses pulling cannons and wagons. Every field and valley within ten miles of the camp fills with the greasy smoke of an army counting its losses and resting before continuing to Knoxville. Each day convalescents eagerly watch the road for their regimental colors. The Frenchmen from the train walk off spewing French insults at everyone. That same day, the Irishman Clay sat next to on the train leaves for his unit.

November 5th, 1862

"Sergeant Miller."

"Yes, sir."

Hightower points an exhausted finger toward empty water barrels next to the surgical tent. In the parlance of Clay's mind, an exhausted finger pointing equates to trust in the young man from Highland. Doctor Hightower points and Clay gets it done. Like wearing a perfectly fitted shirt, he feels comfortable being in charge.

"Get right on it, sir."

Ordering the detail into the back of a wagon, the strongest man Clay has ever met struggles to board the wagon, yet Clay doesn't see it. He's too busy basking in his newfound confidence. Frank, now seated next to Clay, gives a skilled snap of the reins across the backsides of the mules.

Leaving the camp, they enter the road now filled with a brigade of infantry, each regiment moving with its colors in its middle and their colonel at the front. Frank turns the wagon against the stream, his expert wagon skills negotiating through stragglers and the edge of the column. When moving to the beat, an army is a disciplined machine of men moving four abreast, left feet landing at exactly the same time followed quickly by right feet—ninety steps per minute, the fife and drum keeping the cadence. An army at the route step is much looser, its linear form softened by the independent foot falls of each soldier.

Seeing corporals and generals pass with their heads hung low in defeat, like a young peacock eager to show his plumage, Clay stands up in the jostling wagon, searching for a pair of eyes to be impressed by him. A colonel in full military regalia passes. Clay gives a cocky salute. A rut slams Clay almost out of the wagon. The colonel smiles at the young pup's pomposity.

"Best grab hold of somethin," Tennessee laughs.

Dave finds his cousin's actions odd. "Clay, what are you doing?" Another rut almost slams Clay back to his seat beside Frank. "Hold on to something before you go ass over tea kettle."

Clay is determined to show the world his chevrons.

An artillery battery passes. Warm for November, the column shows the effect of the heat and the miles.

"What battery are ya?" Tennessee asks the passing cannon crew.

"Scott's Battery" is the return.

"What regiment is this?" Tennessee asks.

"12ᵗʰ Tennessee."

"Hey, Miller. That's the 12ᵗʰ Tennessee. They're in my brigade." Tennessee explodes in excitement. "Where's the 154th?" he calls back to the column.

A private, the knees on his soiled pants worn through and his feet almost bare, looks to the Tennessean. "What's it to ya?"

"Where's the 154th Tennessee?" he calls again. Before Clay knows it, Tennessee sprints out of the wagon.

"You've not been relieved," Clay yells out.

Tennessee smiles, "Somethin better's come along." He tosses a grand wave and heads toward his regiment's flag.

"Go get em, boy," Milford yells out. "Wish I was joinin ya," he says as he scans the column for his regiment's flag.

Clay shrinks.

"Soon enough we'll be back in our real units," Dave's words bring Clay back to a sad reality.

Naiveté has not been kind to Clay. In his innocence he interpreted the chevrons on his jacket as an oath of allegiance from them. He thought the way the boys accepted his orders meant they respected him. His mind questions the eagerness of Tennessee and Milford wanting to rejoin their units. Just about every detail, no matter how gruesome the task, was done well. *I did more work than any of them. Let them know it too.* Hightower trusted them. Clay did his job well. *Why?*

"Hey, Clay, ya think the 7th be by soon?" Milford asks.

The words smack Clay in the face. The 7th. He hadn't thought about the regiment in a long while. Now a curiosity, not a yearning, more a wonderment has Clay thinking about Alex and Hiram. Are they both still alive or has the decision been made for him? Then he wonders if this new Clay will fit in the old world. Then again, is there a new Clay or a just the same old fool whitewashed. Clay watches Milford scanning the road for the 7th. Only Frank, quietly sitting next to him, shows no signs of wanting to leave him. Leaning deep into his reins, Frank gently guides the mules. The wagon wheels stop a few feet from a stream crowded by butternut and gray soldiers. Before the others can get out of the wagon, Clay splashes to midstream with a ten-gallon barrel in his arms. The water reaching above his ankles, he tips the barrel letting the flow of the water fill the barrel for him. He can hear the others unloading the wagon, but stays focused on what he's doing, avoiding looking at them, knowing they'll leave soon, and he'll have to leave soon too. Then what?

"Hey Frank, what kind a business you doing there?" Dave grunts as he slides another barrel into the stream.

Clay looks to see Frank no longer in the wagon, but squatting in the stream, his bare ass inches from the water. His face distorts as he releases his stool. The greasy water flows downstream to where Clay fills the barrel.

"Frank!"

Frank squeezes in a vain attempt to stop his flow. Pants

gathered about his knees, one hand holding his ass closed, the other trying to keep his clothes from falling in the water, he struggles. "It's passed now." He pulls his pants up.

Clay moves toward him, "How long you been loose?"

"Comes and goes."

Clay has always been one to live inside himself. As a child, he played alone more than with others. Even with Alex and the Highland boys, Clay often preferred time in himself. When Mr. Miller gave hell to Clay's mom, Clay would run off to the woods to pretend he was a valiant knight like those he read about with Julie. Leading armies and saving damsels in distress. To be the hero. To be of something. At the dinner table, Clay often played with his food until Mr. Miller often gave a slap whenever the dreamer's face needed to be brought back to this world. Camp Hightower has been Clay's first taste of reality to his fantasies. Seeing Frank sick, however, changes to a new reality.

Clay looks at Frank's sunken eyes and fragile form. "Blood?

"Last coupla a days."

Clay never noticed Frank going to sinks. He was too busy being important. Too busy trying to please Hightower to notice. A soft hand on Frank's shoulder is an apology for being so self-absorbed. "Best go to the wagon and lie down."

Clay sees the strongest man he has ever known struggle to get into the wagon. Living in Camp Hightower has shown Clay how men die of dysentery—bloody diarrhea spilling down their leg, a growing weakness as the body struggles to keep anything in, next dehydration sets in, then horrible chills, then, finally, an almost welcome death. Seeing a man with the bloody flux is seeing a man shit himself to death. *Damned him.* Clay moves to help Frank into the wagon where he lays him down. Clay's jacket becomes Frank's blanket.

"Let's get him back to Doc Hightower," Dave takes the reins. "Maybe the blue pill will fix him up."

Heading down the bank to fetch a barrel, Clay sees a threadbare soldier filling his canteen, not from the creek, but from the barrel.

"Hey, what the hell are you doing?" The soldier ignores Clay. "You, jack-a-nape. We didn't fill that for your soul benefit." Clay begins a movement toward him, throwing his shoulders back and his chest out like a threatened peacock. Like a boy pretending to be a man, Clay fabricates a reason to thrash the soldier. Like a kid caught being what he's not, the soldier looks up.

"Be about your business, hospital rat."

The words slam Clay to a halt. Shame replaces compensating rage. Fantasy exposed, Clay's mind swims between two positions of life—peacock or hospital rat. *Doesn't he know about Shiloh, the hospital, infection, my cheek just healing?* The soldier lifts his canteen. Looking Clay in the eye, he drinks. He's not a big man and looks well-worn, but as usual, Clay is as weak as a child before an abusive stepfather.

"For your information, I've been healing from Shiloh," Clay stumbles out a weak validation.

"That was April." The soldier returns the cork to the canteen then splashes across the creek to his regiment.

"Shit."

He stands exposed. Is this ragged Reb right? It was April and Clay is just now returning to the regiment. Sure, he didn't want to get back to the regiment right away. He begins to wonder why. *What is because I was still too damaged, or was it to avoid choosing between Alex or Hiram?* Better said, was he avoiding choosing between what he is and what he wants to be? Highland is who is he. College, and now here is who he wants to be. He can't find the answer. Instead he finds a rage that grows from not knowing and feeling like what that Reb defined him as.

Clay hefts the full weight of the barrel of water. From the shoulder, he tosses it into the wagon where Dave and Milford feel the brute force of it.

"Get that damn barrel in the wagon. Tired of doing all the work," Clay yells.

"What the hell's his problem," Milford whispers to Dave.

"Shh."

"Let's get back to camp," Sergeant Miller barks at his detail.

Dave whips the mule. Milford steams about the way Clay treated them. Frank shivers. Clay sits alone. On the march to Shiloh, Clay saw a soldier, a kid really, purposely smash out his four front teeth so he couldn't tear a musket cartridge. Can't tear the cartridge, can't load a musket was a coffee cooler's way of avoiding battle. Clay found him disgusting. While that yellow bastard walked back to Corinth with his bleeding toothless grin, Clay marched to a bullet. The memory of laying on that battlefield, in that darkening hollow, using his slouch hat to staunch the blood, rain and blood dripping into his eyes, running in his mouth, his blood, his gore, in his mouth. *I wasn't a hospital rat then.* The sound of the Yankee gunboats tossing shell after shell into the wood where he lay made him feel as if they had a personal desire to smash him beyond the hole in his cheek where he heard air wheeze through when he exhaled. His jaw crackling whenever he moved it. But that was April. *Yeah, I'm a hospital rat.*

The wagon stops in front of the tent where Clay sees Doctor Hightower stretching his back.

"Sergeant, get those barrels unloaded. I've just run out of water. My instruments are unwashed."

Sir, can you check on Frank?" Clay brooches. "Afraid he's got the flux pretty bad."

Hightower responds in the voice of his official position, "White men first," but he quickly hands Clay a blue pill before returning to his work.

Water unloaded, Dave and Milford head back to their camp while Clay does everything he physically can to help Uncle Frank. He places Frank in the bed of the wagon so he won't have to sleep on the ground. He even steals straw from a hospital bed, filling the bed of the wagon with it. Clay covers the man he loves as a father in as much warmth and comfort as he can provide. He looks at the red eyes and graying skin poking dark amongst the blonde straw and wool blanket. He tries to feel. He tries to cry. He tries to feel compassion. He stands silent in front of a locked door without a key. No matter how much he tries, Clay doesn't feel anything. Mechanical support is all Clay can give so he gives it in heaps. Clay wonders what's wrong with him. Why can't he cry? Clay hands him his canteen. Frank barely drinks, then, with an appreciative nod, he turns his face to free Clay.

For the rest of the night, Clay lies below the wagon listening to the dying man above him. A dozen times he helps Frank relieve himself. Not enough.

In the morning Clay returns to their campsite to get help from Dave and Milford only to find them gone. They took everything with them, even Old Thunder. Nothing left to do, he goes to the only place in this world he might find help. Wrapping Frank in the blanket, Clay and Frank head out to find the 7th. Moving past the arbor, Clay sees Captain Hightower at yet another wagon load of wounded. With a nod and a slight bow, Clay offers his silent thank you to a noble man, but Captain Hightower is too busy to see him.

Chapter Seven

November 14th, 1862

Clay and a weak-legged Frank moves toward Chalmers' Brigade and the 7th Mississippi. Finding the regiment, they move to the regimental headquarters where Clay hears the distinct voice of Alex's brother. In front of the colonel's tent, Tucker Current stands guard.

"Clay!" Tucker exhorts, "Oh man, we thought you was dead." He vigorously shakes Clay's hand.

The commotion draws the colonel out of his tent. "What's this?"

Thinking the colonel is reacting to the stripes on Clay's jacket, "Sir, Captain Hightower made me a sergeant?"

"Clay Miller back from to us, colonel, sir," Tucker beams while the colonel looks Clay up and down.

"Not sure to whom you speak, mister. What is your rank in this regiment?

Crestfallen, Clay responds, "Private."

"Then that is what you are. Make sure to remove those stripes as soon as you get to camp."

"Yes, sir." Clay pulls his knife out and removes the chevrons in front of the colonel. With the last one cut off, they fall into the dirt.

Seeing Frank, the colonel addresses Clay, "The pet niggers are over by the commissary. Send yours there, then get to your company."

Before Clay can react, Frank looks at him, "Nigga knows where he belongs." And with that, he moves unsteadily toward a herd of commissary wagons and a half-dozen black faces.

"Let's get you to the Hogg Mess," Tucker takes Clay toward the regiment's company streets. Set up just like at Corinth except with more tattered tents and tattered men, Clay immediately notices how empty each street is. In Corinth, each company carried almost a hundred men. The streets he passes here carry less than half that number. Tucker notices Clay's focus.

"We lost a few since we last seen ya."

Clay's mind races to the faces that matter to him. Alex. Will Alex stand tall by the campfire when he arrives? Hiram. Will Hiram be leaning against a tent pole reading? Clay wonders how he will feel when he sees—or doesn't see—them. Since Shiloh, Clay has fended for himself without Alex's protection or Hiram's tutoring. Clay smiles a bit as he reflects on how well he has done since Shiloh. The sergeant stripes proved that. Deep down, Clay hopes they're alive, but is not as excited to see them as much as he wishes he were still at Camp Hightower. In spite of losing Tennessee and the rest, he will miss the value he felt there. Yet, he knows he had to leave. Seeing Frank disappear into the sable crowd gives Clay a moment of validation for leaving the camp. *He'll be taken care of better by his kind—more than I can help him.*

"Yer old Frank looks mighty sick," Tucker engages.

"Yea," followed by the silence of reflection on the two worlds waiting for him.

Silence is not a friend of Tucker, so he jabbers about his itch, then how he almost bought the farm at Perryville. He tells the story of how he took a chicken from a pregnant nigger woman he met on the retreat, and how the Hogg Mess ate like kings thanks to him. Clay grabs onto a phrase he's not heard before.

"What's a Hogg Mess?"

Tucker begins, "Alex named us. He said, "Let's call ourselves Hogg Mess since we livin like pigs and we are a mess, he said." Tucker laughs at the idea. "Well, anyway, me, Alex, Stewart, Rut, and your Hiram have formed a mess. The Hogg Mess. Two g's since we so special."

Hearing their names lets him know they're alive. Hearing their names reminds him of the apology he needs to give. The choice yet finalized.

Tucker continues to explain how the five of them help each other with rations, duties, and whatever each other needs help with. "Believe it, we work pretty good together. Even Alex and your boy Hiram is getting along fairly good. That may change now that ya'll back."

Shocked, Clay asks, "How?"

"Well, you know Alex. Food has always been his friend. Well, it turns out Hiram can cook, and right proper. Said his servant taught him. That sealed the deal between those two." Tucker points to a row of tents just ahead. "There's the company."

Approaching the company fire, Clay sees Hiram bending over a frying pan while Alex watches intently. Clay's steps accelerate.

"Hey, Hoggs, come and see what Tucker dragged up," Tucker calls the boys over.

Alex sees Clay first. Rushing forward, he surrounds Clay in a bear hug. "Clay!"

Out comes Rut from the nearest tent. Rut, the oldest of the mess by six years, is a good guy who quietly does his business and thanks no man for the privilege. They shake hands. On the day Clay joined the company, he walked past Will Rutledge and his four children playing in their front yard, where he found himself drawn to the giggling of the small boys and the chuckle of a father enjoying his crop. His eyes watched the father chasing happy children around an unkempt yard. Like a bear with cubs, Rut fell down so his cubs could pounce. Tugging and squeezing, his children tried to flip him onto his back when the oldest boy, maybe ten, pulled Rut's hair so hard the father winced in pain. Clay tensed in anticipation of the beating, and was about to turn from a scene he knew only too well, when he saw a father's hands gently release the boy's grip.

Rut kissed his son on the forehead. As a soldier, Rut lives without a filter on his actions or words. One never knows what he'll say or do. His unfettered openness is endearing and entertaining.

Next, George Stewart offers a formal, rather disdainful handshake. The uneasy rivalry between the two has not quieted.

"Hey, Clay, you look like a fatted calf. How you so plump? And well appointed?" Alex inspects his friend.

Alex is right. By comparison to the mess, Clay is fleshy and well dressed. Tucker looks the scarecrow, a living symbol of the rough times the army had in Kentucky. Alex is still strong looking, but his shoulders stoop just enough to be noticed by someone who's been absent. Stewart's beard is beginning to show grey. Only Hiram, although more sloppy with his muddy boots and bent-up visor on his kepi, looks more stout than ever, his electric eyes still glowing. Finally, Hiram offers a handshake. Clay places his left hand over the bond cementing his joy at seeing Hiram again. Alex notices it.

Alex separates the handshake, "You'll be needing to pitch into a tent. We have ourselves two. One has me and Tuck while the other has George, Rut and that one." Alex points a finger at Hiram.

Two tents. Two versions of Clay. Alex or Hiram? Highland or College? He wishes he were back tending hospital beds.

Rut spouts, "Where ya been?"

Hiram moves closer. "We heard you died in the hospital."

"Thought sure you bought it," Alex says, blocking Hiram from Clay's view.

Tattoo, the music ending a day in camp, tells soldiers to get to sleep.

"You stay with us, Clay. Plenty of room," Alex says ushering him into his tent, and Clay is thankful Alex made the decision for him. Clay doesn't want to think, or decide, or act. Hiram goes into his tent with Stewart and Rut.

Exhausted, Clay prepares a bed for himself in the tent. Hoping Frank is warm with the blanket, Clay covers up with his jacket while Tucker and Alex burrow themselves into their kit. Then, for a delicious moment, the silence of familiars fills the tent.

"Who dropped their ass?" The tent explodes in laughter. It's good to be back.

Sleep falls over the camp.

The warmth of a nice day gives way to the winds of an upcoming cold snap that flows between the ground and the canvas where Clay's toes lie exposed in socks that have long lost their integrity. Clay wiggles and flexes his toes to keep the blood flowing. Using a trick he learned back home, Clay takes his jacket and wraps it around his feet. Mr. Miller didn't go for wasting good firewood to heat the house, so Clay learned to make himself warm. Feet toastily wrapped in his jacket, Clay pulls at the blanket covering Alex. Careful to take only half, his eyes grow heavy and his mind begins to relax. It's been a good day.

Only Frank's condition worries Clay, but there's nothing he can do tonight.

Five minutes or two hours, time is lost to the night. A snoring Tucker doesn't wake up Clay. Alex dropping his ass doesn't faze him. 'Never drink before you go to bed, son,' his mother's lesson forgotten by a young Clay who always had to go to the outhouse in the middle of the night. Clay has to relieve himself.

The urgency of the need has Clay leaving the tent in his socks where he discovers a light snow has been falling for a while. Too late to go back for his shoes, he quickly moves behind the tent to where a camp guard walks the tree line, too busy trying to stay warm to notice a tiptoeing fool. Moving into the trees, Clay begins to relieve himself. His chest exhales slowly and relief comes across his face as he enjoys a simple pleasure. He watches snowflakes fall from the blackness to the growing whiteness of the ground. He continues to go. A snowflake lands on his nose. He goes. A nip of cold introduces itself, nibbling on the back of his hand. He goes. A snowflake lands on eyelid. The flow shows no sign of ebbing. Cold. "Hurry, damned it!" His feet chill. Socks absorb the wintry blend. "I can't wait any longer." He doesn't completely finish.

Sprinting back to the tents, Clay knows he's been out too long to ever find enough heat under half of Alex's blanket. Seeing a row of fires being cared for by Neil Current, a cousin to Alex and Tucker, Clay moves to the one nearest his tent. Sitting down, Clay places his frosted toes close to the fire, and in moments the numbness of the cold is replaced by the feel of hot embers barely inches from his socks. He pulls back ever so slightly when Neil comes up to drop a small pile of firewood next to Clay.

"How long you been on duty, Neil?"

"Bout an hour. Not too bad, keeps me warm." Neil goes to take a sip from his canteen. Pulling at the cork, he can't remove it.

"Frozen. Well, what'll ya know? Oh well, guess I wasn't thirsty anyway," Neil says as he moves to stoke another fire.

The fire makes a better blanket than any Clay left in the tent, so he curls up as close to the fire as possible and soon falls asleep.

Predawn, the fire which lulled Clay to sleep is now a pile of white ash, except for a small red glow. Fire can be rekindled. Wiping the sleep and soot from his eyes, Clay begins rebuilding the fire with what's available. Wetting his fingers to protect them from the hot ends of sticks whose centers burned up last night, he makes them into a small pile; then he leans in, his face almost touching the pile. Blowing ever so gently, his wind turns embers into sparks. He does it again. The sparks become new born flames. He works harder and for that, flames lick heat into the cold air. It's going to be a good day. Snuggling up to a fire, now very much alive, he warms his hands.

The movement of a tent flap has Clay looking to a blanket-covered Hiram moving toward the fire. Clay looks for the glow of friendship. Cold. Quickly, he piles all the wood he has on the fire. The heat draws Hiram closer. Silence.

February 1861

Returning from class, Clay enters their room excited to tell Hiram what he's learned today, something Clay has been doing more and more since the night he brought home Emerson. The light of learning has decided, by conscious union, to burn inside Clay. Clay's mind has grown powerful thanks in large part to Hiram.

"Clay, you have a letter from your father."

The deep furrows in Clay's forehead and his heated complexion tell Hiram that Clay is in pain. Clay opens the letter.

I purchased a woodlot that needs clearing. Frank's too old to clear it. It's time for you to return to Highland.

Your mother passed last week. The doctor says she died of melancholy. We buried her yesterday.

G. Miller

"Stay," Hiram encourages.

"I can't."

Light leaves the room. Two days later Clay stands over his mother's grave. He pounds the earth in anger at her for leaving him. It's cold.

"Get cold last night? "Clay's best attempt at rekindling the friendship.

Hiram stands silent.

Clay tries, "I see Alex is still a pain in the ass."

Nothing.

"It's nice and warm by the fire," Clay opens his hand to the open space next to him.

Hiram sits, his eyes locked on the flames licking at the air. Clay finds a small twig and tosses it into the fire in the hopes Hiram will look at him. It works. Hiram wipes his nose with a leather covered finger. From off in distance, the fleshiest confederate Clay has ever seen walks up. Baby fat and pink cheeks tell of a fresh fish.

"Mind ifn I shar yer fire?" The big man plops between Clay and Hiram. "Man, I never been cold my entire life," he whines.

Seeing Hiram cloaked in a blanket makes him feel better about his plight. Seeing Clay sitting in shirt sleeves has him in wonderment.

"Ain't you cold? Man, I bout froze to death back in dat tent."

"Why didn't you sleep by a fire?" Clay asks, pointing to the fire in front of the fat man's tent. The big man offers a defeated sigh at the epiphany of the obvious, then heads back to his frozen tent. Confused, Clay looks to Hiram.

"Better cold than admit the foolishness," Hiram says as he moves toward his tent. Turning back for just a moment, "Not everyone thinks like you, Clay," Hiram smiles. Fire rekindled.

Chapter Eight

November 16th, 1862

Days of formations and fatigue duty returns Clay to the army rhythm he was beginning to understand before his Shiloh. Unfortunately, Clay has seen Frank only once since arriving, and that was when Frank was helping the commissary sergeant with rations. A shared nod was the best they could do. Clay's glad to see Frank with other men of color as Frank was the Miller's only slave and hardly ever went off the farm. Living together in seeming harmony with their songs filling their labors, Clay hopes Frank is happy.

Clay shivers and pries his eyes open to an empty tent. No Alex fouling the air. No Tucker spreading out across the tent floor. Taking a deep breath, Clay begins to enjoy the aloneness when shouting and laughing calls his attention outside the tent. With Alex's coverlet wrapped around his shoulders, he opens the tent flap. SMACK!

"How's it taste?" Stewart gloats.

SMACK! Stewart receives a white missile to his chest.

"Hey, leave him alone," Alex comes up like a snowy knight. "Till I get a shot at him." SMACK! Clay spits snow.

Last night the sky dropped six inches of snow and this morning thousands of confederate soldiers become children again, the sky full of snowballs. SMACK! Hiram takes one from Alex. Hiram returns fire with an angry throw that misses from ten feet away. Hiram seethes at his inability to get Alex a good one.

Tucker told Clay the two were getting along. Clay sees the opposite as Alex torments Hiram every time Hiram comes near Clay.

Clay watches Hiram take a deep breath to clear his anger. Bending down, Hiram finds a walnut-sized stone. Packing the stone in snow, he fires a snowball that emasculates; Alex falls, his hands holding the pain in his crotch. Hiram laughs. Clay smiles. Alex gets up in a rage. *This will be ugly.* Snowball in hand, Alex charges Hiram. Just inches from contact, Alex stops. Snowball on high plane, he stares down into Hiram's defiant eyes. Alex smiles. Hiram gets a white wash. Clay laughs on the outside while on the inside, even though the moment diffused itself, he grieves for not stepping up to protect Hiram. Hiram steams away.

And so the battle goes. Stewart hits Hiram. Tucker hits Stewart. Alex leaves Hiram alone, instead going after Clay. Mississippi boys rarely see snow, and never this amount, so the fun continues. Needham Braird, the town curmudgeon and oldest man in the company, comes out of his tent to a fusillade. He retreats behind canvas.

Even some officers become kids at heart. Inside the captain's tent Clay's company commander puts on his sword belt. Peeking out of his tent flap to make sure his men are not lying in wait, he comes out into the open, draws his sword on high plane then bellows, "Let's get those Milford Rifle boys." The company cheers.

"Fall in," commands Stewart and in moments the company forms two ranks faster than for any drill or fatigue duty.

"Captain, the company is formed," Sergeant Stewart offers with an over exaggerated martial salute.

The captain returns the salutes. Turning to the company with the dramatics of the lead actor in a cheap theatre troupe, he orders, "Load."

There are two kinds of men here, the ones who put rocks in their snowballs and those who don't. Alex does. Hiram does. Stewart doesn't. Clay doesn't. Hands full, they reform in time for the command, "Forward March." As if on parade, the company advances on a row of tents where the Milford Rifles mill about, unsuspecting of the approaching avalanche.

"Double Quick Time," the captain orders. Seeing the charging line makes the Milford boys scramble helter skelter. Their movement reminds Clay of Shiloh. Most run off. Some stay and fight.

"Fire at will. Commence Firing," the captain commands. A volley of snowballs explodes on the Milford men who dare to stand their ground.

"Just like Shiloh," Alex shouts.

"Not the second day," Needham Braird reminds.

Highland men have never thought much of Milford boys who are river people, and of a sort many look down on, though Clay's low station keeps him from judging anyone.

"CHARGE!" the captain shouts.

Grey uniforms intermix; snow or clenched fists the weapons of choice. Clay searches for a target. Alex smashes snow into a tow-headed boy's face. Clay sees Milford in the act of putting a stone in a snowball. Clay fires. Milford spits snow. Alex fires at the common target. Stewart, Rut, Tucker, and Hiram smells blood in the water so they fire too. Milford collapses in surrender. The Hogg Mess unknowingly help Clay punish Milford for leaving Clay back at Camp Hightower. Clay is reloading when he feels a smash into his right cheek, the rock core smashing into his scar. He falls to the ground, hand checking his old wound. His face hurts, but no blood. Clay opens his eyes to a smiling Hiram. Payback. Clay knows he deserves it.

Just as Clay is about to return fire, General Chalmers rides up, "What regiment is this?"

"Sir, 7th Mississippi, Company E," Clay salutes.

"Good. We're about to form the brigade. Time to go after them Tennessee sons-a-bitches." Chalmers looks like a cat about to get the canary. "Form your regiment."

For the next two hours, a brigade-on-brigade battle sees flags flying, bands playing, and officers exhorting their men to great deeds of bravery. Snowball charges and counter charges across the parade field and amongst the tents lasts until exhaustion renders both sides too spent to go on. Some units march back to their bivouacs while other units dissolve either cheering their victory or threatening revenge on their betters of that day. Scores of wounded nurse bloody noses and black eyes. Physically spent, Clay and the rest return to camps where their wet uniforms and cold hands make them shiver. Those with extra clothing sprint to their tents to exchange wet for dry while men like Clay head to fires.

Clay places his wet socks on a stick then waves them slowly over the fire. Alex joins in with a soaked shirt. Tucker does the same. Needham Braird has come to the fire to dry his pants, everyone careful not to look his way for fear of seeing what they don't want to see. Each man watches as their clothing smokes like the Christmas ham while Hiram sits smug and dry next to Stewart who also had extra clothing. They're there for the entertainment. Once in a while a piece of clothing falls into the flame, all but the victim laughing.

"Oh shit." HOT! Dropped. Hot! Dropped. "Got it. Or what's left of it." The cloth smolders rings of orange. "At least it's dry," laughs Alex as he surveys the crisp edges of his only shirt.

Cold, half-clothed men desperately try to stave off misery, and yet they laugh. A blanket placed on a messmate's back, help saving a burning sock, a tease, and a laugh are what comrades do. They grow quiet gazing into the hypnotic glow of the fire. Clay begins to think about Frank and how he's doing when Rut's random thought breaks the moment.

"Heard we're goin to be shipped to Virginia. Gonna take Washington City."

Campfires are pulpits for gossip. Hiram shares what he knows, "My father works with Mr. Judah Benjamin in the war department, and he says there's talk of all the Mississippi soldiers being sent to Vicksburg to join Stephenson's division."

Alex gives a, "Hell yeah! A Mississippi-only army is what this war needs." Pointing in the direction of the Tennesseans they just fought. He adds, "God knows, they ain't got the sand."

While his peers strategize like generals, Clay again thinks about Frank and the slaves brought into the army to do the manual labor their masters find distasteful. Some of the officers have their servants making supper, polishing leather, and tending horses. Clay, unknowingly, gave his up to the regiment's commissary. From behind the campfire Stewart returns.

"Fall in for three-days rations."

The men sprint to their respective tents to grab haversacks, and in moments every man stands in formation, ready for whatever the army found to feed them. Clay and Alex race to the formation like school boys when Clay finds Frank kneeling over a ground cloth covered in piles of rations.

"Frank!"

Frank stays on his business and Clay respects the seriousness of what he's doing so he stands silent, glad to see him up and about, hoping he is doing well. He watches Frank put small slabs of salt pork on each pile of cornmeal, one for each member of the company. Next, he adds the delicacies that are never plentiful enough for all, but a feast for a few. Luck will decide who gets the extra. He puts an Irish potato on two piles, four piles have a parsnip, and one has a small poke bag of corn coffee. Every man stares at the delicacies and prays to God for the parsnip, potato, or coffee. It's here that Clay notices a tremor in Frank's movements, like an inner chill torments his every movement. Finally Frank turns his face to Clay. Blood shot eyes and the same hollowed cheeks tell Clay all he needs to know about Frank's condition.

"That'll do boy," Stewart orders Frank away to stand in the distance.

In order to make a fair distribution of rations, Stewart stands looking at the rations with his back to the formation. Corporal Jones has his back to the rations. Stewart, using his ramrod, points to a pile of food.

"Who shall have this?" Stewart asks.

"Current, Tucker," the Corporal Jones reads.

"Who shall have this," the ramrod points to a potato pile. The men tense. Clay moves his focus to the rations.

"Current, Alex." Cheers and groans.

Piles randomly chosen, names randomly given.

"Who shall have this?"

"Miller, Clay."

Clay moves toward a pile of food without delicacy when, out of the corner of his eye, he sees Frank sink shoulder and face into the mud. Clay rushes to him and lifts Frank's face up. His greyed whiskers have collected mud around his chin; his eyes show an emotion never before shown. Fear. A lightning bolt cracks the wall within Clay. Like a leak in a dam, emotions seep from the crack. Fear cries out, Why? Anger yells out, No! Clay worries about falling apart completely. *No time for this*, his mind regains control.

"Can I gets a drink?" Frank asks.

Clay offers his canteen.

"Who shall have this?" Stewart continues with the rations.

"Stringer, Hiram." A parsnip awaits.

Hiram places the parsnip on Clay's pile. Not to be outdone, Alex puts his potato on the same pile.

The formation dismisses with Stewart telling the company they are marching out in the morning. Alex brings Clay's rations to him and says, "Maybe Frank might do with a bite of parsnip."

"Thank you, Alex."

Hiram fumes while Clay takes a bite of the parsnip and begins to chew. Taking the cud from his mouth, he opens Frank's mouth.

"Chew."

"You better get him to a doctor. He can't even chew for

himself," Alex tells Clay.

Moving Frank's mouth up and down like priming a pump, Clay tries to get Frank to chew.

"Come on, Frank, chew this. It'll help."

Frank slowly begins to, if not for his own good, for Clay. Clay feels Frank's forehead. It's burning hot. From deep within Frank a grumbling sound ends in Clay smelling Frank's dysentery.

"Sorry, Mista Clay," Frank mutters.

Black man or not, Clay decides. Pulling Frank up by his blanket, Clay has him standing, but just barely. "Let's go see Hightower. He'll get you right."

Ignoring the vileness leaking out, Clay puts his arm around Frank's fragile form. Practically carrying the strongest man Clay has ever known, each step is a labor of two feet fighting to keep four moving. Mustering up every ounce of strength in his body, Clay moves the two out of camp and on the road to Hightower when he feels his strength giving way. Clay's mind hears the plea of every muscle crying out to quit. Frank has helped as much as he can, but he's done. Half dragged, half carried, Frank goes limp.

A selfish voice cries out in Clay. He wants to run away from the vile smell that has him on the verge of vomiting. Most of all, he wants to run away from the emotions spewing from the crack in the protective wall he built around himself. Looking for help, there is no one. There never is. *Shit.*

"Come on, Uncle Frank. Use your legs."

Frank attempts to put weight on a leg, but fails to right himself. Clay feels Frank is giving up. *Frank can't quit. He can't.*

"Bullshit. That's not your best effort," Clay explodes. "Stand up, damn you!" Defiance glares at Clay as Frank manages an unsteady stand. He weakly pushes his boy aside.

"I cans stands up," he begins to put one foot in front of the other.

Wobbly, yet defiant, he moves. Clay finds hope. Another step and life leaves. Falling in a heap, Frank's body becomes dead weight to Clay's attempt to get him standing. The sound of a wagon makes Clay fight to get Frank out of the roadway. Clay knows no teamster will steer around the body of a black man. Getting to the side of the road, Clay covers Frank as the wagon passes without comment or notice. Frank shits again.

Looking around for something, anything, Clay searches for relief. Still a quarter mile to Hightower. Clay knows they'll never make it before dark. A chill moves across the valley, chasing the embers of a sun that won't return for a dozen hours. Searching for shelter, Clay sees a farmer's wall just off this side of road. Ignoring the mental and physical exhaustion that has made Clay feel as weak as Frank, he pulls Frank to it. Panting from the supreme effort, Clay leans against the irregularly placed rocks to catch his breath. His body wants to quit. His mind wants to run away from the filth that has forever stained him. Wagons and soldiers canter past on their way to camp before dark.

To protect Frank from the night Clay places him parallel to the wall. He puts his jacket under Frank's head. A barely audible thank you tells Clay he has to do more. Frank's beginning to shake uncontrollably. Seeing an oak tree just feet from them, Clay races to pull off kindling for a fire. Bending, ripping, trying to pull, their pliability mocks Clay's efforts for there is too much life in the branches for it to give itself to a fire. Desperate, he loses fingernails as he attempts to tear off bark. *If only I had Old Thunder*, Clay's mind sprints to when he could fell a tree like this with ease. Frustrated, Clay punches the tree. Again, Again. *Damn it! Why?* His brain cries out.

"Clay," the feeble voice calls.

"Here, Frank," Clay returns. "Maybe a drink'll help."

Frank refuses the canteen. The light fades fast yet Clay keeps fighting. He notices some twigs and leaves piled against the rock wall. Hands become a blur of collecting the driest leaves he can find. He then takes the driest twigs and places them on the leaves. A faint sound draws his attention back; a half gurgle, half choke. He sees Frank trying to say something.

"What is it?" Clay leans in.

With his last ounce of life, Frank clears his throat, "You a good boy."

Absorbed with the idea of a fire, Clay escapes into what he knows. Refusing the words and the emotions they bring, he reaches into his haversack where he finds a candle. If he can light the candle, then he can light the leaves, then the branches, then the wet wood. If he can keep Frank warm. Digging for his match safe. Frustration explodes, "Where are my matches?" No matches. SHIT! A black hand pulls Clay close.

"Yous gonna be okay."

The wall releases the flood, "Not without you."

Looking to the road, Clay sees a mess of soldiers heading back to camp. He sees Milford among the group. Hope returns.

"Milford, I need a match?" Clay calls out while pointing to Frank.

Looking toward the stone fence, Milford sees a shadow of a man wrapped in a coverlet. "Sick pard?"

"Trying to get him to hospital, but we can't make it tonight," Clay sees one of the group carrying two chickens by the neck.

"Is it one of your pards?" Milford looks into the twilight to get a look at the downed man. He digs in his pocket for his match safe.

Clay pulls out $1.50 from his pocket, the last of his money. He turns to the man with the chickens. If he can fry up that chicken, it might give Frank strength. "Will you take this for one of those chickens?"

"Fair price," Milford's messmate responds.

Milford looks closer at the dark form, "Is that your nigger Frank?"

"Just one match," Clay cries out. "Just one chicken."

Milford now holds the matches like a trophy. "No damn

way. These chickens and my matches is for white folks."

Clay charges, fighting to get the matches from Milford. He rips at Milford to get just one match. The other men smash Clay to the ground.

"Guess you and your boys shouldn't have hit me with those snowballs there, Clay." The words kick Clay in the stomach.

Laughing, Milford and his mess head to camp while Clay pulls himself up from the road. Quietly. Respectfully. Lovingly, he lays down next to Frank to hold him close, to share his heat with the only father figure he has ever known, the first person who saw value in him. In spite of the smell and shit pouring from Frank, Clay will stay like this all night. He'll stay with Frank for as long as necessary. It's at this moment Clay realizes a feeling he's never known.

"I love you."

Frank leans deeper into the boy, and Clay embraces him. Slowly Frank's shivering subsides and his breathing shallows. Clay too slows. He falls asleep.

July 1854

A black man tends to the reddened face of a boy beaten by his stepfather. Tears streak the swollen cheek of the kid. The boy leans into the black man's chest and cries. Black hands hold him tight.

The fife and drum wake up the camp to a beautiful fall

morning, the cold wind of last night giving way to pink skies and sunshine.

From his tent, Alex moves to the fire where Hiram warms his hands.

Hiram charges, "Alex, what you did yesterday was low, even for you. Low." Hiram steams. "I don't care about you taking credit for the parsnip. That's not it."

"Clay didn't come back last night," Alex tells Hiram.

Hiram stops. A higher order trumps all the petty animosity between the two. "He didn't?"

Stewart comes out of the tent to the two men facing each other, and expecting what's been brewing since spring to explode, he sprints between them. Before he speaks, Alex says, "George, Clay isn't back yet." Alex's face shows the same concern as Hiram's.

Stewart sees the truce. "You both head to the hospital and see if he got his nigger there. Find Frank and you'll find Miller."

Both men nod in agreement, and they quickly head down the road to Camp Hightower. Passing the Milford Rifles camp, they smell frying chicken. About a half mile out they come to a farmer's wall, and next to the wall, near a tree that refused to give up its life, they see a man stooped over the quiet form of another.

While Hiram and Alex bury Frank under loose field stones, Clay heads to a stream to scrub Frank's shit off his uniform and the tears from his face.

Chapter Nine

November 15ᵗʰ, 1862

Clay watches sparks pop from a pine log newly tossed into the fire, its red glow trying to warm a man as cold as the day. Lost, not in thought, just lost, clenched in his right hand is a letter to his mother.

November 13ᵗʰ, 1862

Dear Mother,

I now write you a few lines but with deep regret. I am well at this time but I am sorry to say that Frank is dead. Alex and Hiram buried Frank as best they could. I tried to save him. I tried to help him. I wasn't enough.

It is getting late and I am writing by fire light.

Your son, Clay

Clay pushes the letter deep into the fire, telling himself, "The dead can't read."

November 20ᵗʰ, 1862

Sergeant Stewart moves along a well-worn trail used by confederate soldiers on the way to their picket line. Even though the Yankees are tucked in for the winter miles from here, Sergeant Stewart pushes vigilance and duty. Behind him the detail follows in single file. Stopping at a post, he relieves the previous picket with two of his.

"Alex. Make sure you keep an eye out down that open field."

"Ain't no Yanks within ten miles of us," Alex complains.

Ignoring him, Stewart makes a decision bigger than the war. "Hiram, you too."

"I aint partial to spending my shift with him, George. Give me Clay, "Alex pleads.

Stewart snaps his response, "Miller will have a solo post tonight. You two stay here. And stay alert."

As Stewart moves to the next post, Hiram and Alex watch a quiet Clay move past without looking to his friends. Sometimes what a person doesn't do can be as alarming as what a person does.

"Odd," Hiram says as he watches Clay move off.

"What?"

"He knows we hate each other." Hiram sits down behind the earthwork.

"I don't hate you. Never have."

Hiram's mind recalls the abuse. He slams his musket

down, "Then why have you been the bane of my existence from the first moment I joined this crapfest of a company?"

"Crapfest. Rather vulgar," Alex taunts the educated man when he realizes what he needs to do. "Really. I thought you were smart an' all."

Like a dog hearing a new sound, Hiram tilts his head at the idea that Alex doesn't hate him. Never has.

"Why do you call me 'City Threads' unless to taunt me?"

"Well, you do wear them."

Hiram finds the logic absurd. He finds a worse proof, "Ripping up my books?"

"Only after you threw them away."

Hiram finds an example that most upsets him, "Taking credit for the parsnip?"

"I wasn't trying to take credit for your parsnip," Alex is becoming perturbed. "I was just trying to help out Clay and Ole Frank. For shitsake, there weren't time to laud over the ownership of a damn parsnip."

"Keeping Clay from me?"

Alex settles in next to Hiram. "When Clay came back from college, he was different. Not smarter, we always knew he was the smartest one. He was just different. He became bigger than Highland. Like we was too small for him. I guess I felt I was too small for him." Alex pulls out a chuck of corn pone and begins to chew. "When we joined the army, it was perfect. We got him away from Ole Man Miller, and he and I chummed around just like when we was kids. I watched out fer him, and he was that loyal friend a man is lucky to have once in a lifetime." Alex hands Hiram a chuck of corn pone. "When you came around, I thought sure I'd lose him to you complete. So I got in the way."

"You ostracized me for being Clay's friend." Hiram understands. Clay is a friend that only comes around once in a lifetime. "I guess I was jealous of you two as well. You have a history that I can never compete with." Hiram turns to Alex, "He chose you over me twice. Wasn't that enough?

"Jealous too, I guess. You two got something him and me ain't. I ain't changin anytime soon. I ain't growin. This is who I am and always will be. This time next year, I'll be the same Alex. And you two will be somethin more. And there it is. Some folks grow and others don't. Can't have both."

The clarity of the words strikes Hiram deep. He wants to tell Alex that what he just said is the most genuine human statement he has ever heard. "Glad he has you."

"Glad he has you too," Alex says, leaving the moment to collect kindling for a new fire.

Hiram understands nothing else needs to be said. He asks Alex, "What are you doing?"

"Gonna brew up some chicory. Want some?"

Hiram responds to the olive branch. "I have coffee."

"Of course, you do."

In a few minutes they have a small fire going and water

about to the boil. The silence of clarity fills the picket post. Now that both understand each other, rivals can become allies. Their thoughts turn to their friend. Since Frank died, both men have done their best to keep Clay company. Today, he will be alone.

"You thinkin' 'bout Clay?"

"Yes."

Alex throws a stick into the darkness. "Damned Stewart paying Clay back for lovin Julie. That's why he has us out here, and Clay by hisself. He knows. Yea, he knows." Alex pulls the cup of boiling water from the fire. "Leavin Clay alone is bout the same as handing him a loaded pistol. Dead by morning, I say. Damn that Stewart anyway."

Hiram takes the cup, and from a small sack, pours a friendly amount of real coffee into the water. "He'll be there when we get back."

"How the hell can ya say that? You seen him. Him lyin' there with that 'I-don't-give-a-shit' look on his face, and that cold stare he's got whenever life gets too much for him. I tell you, I seen that stare before, like he ain't in his own body, but somewheres else. Someplace distant." Alex throws another stick, "Never as bad as this."

"No time for riddles, Alex. What do you mean?"

"I seen that blank stare before, back when we was kids. Clay was the kinda kid who would laugh till he cried. His spirit was light and full. Till old man Miller begun to beat it out of him. Not long after his ma married the old man."

"You mean, Mr. Miller isn't his actual father?"

I thought you was his friend," Alex says, narrowing his eyes, "What the hell. How don't you know that?" His hand clenches tight around his coffee cup.

"Clay kept his past his past. He never wanted to share where he came from. And I respected his decision."

Hiram's explanation calms Alex. "Yea, that makes sense. He never told us about his life in Michigan either. Just that he and his ma had to move down by us." Alex extends a hand, "Sorry for that outburst, Hiram. I've been watchin' out for him since I first met him."

April 1853

The new kid moves down an unfamiliar farm lane toward town. Innocent blue eyes scan this new world of southern farms and southern nature when a snake side-winds across the road in front of him. Curious, the boy moves closer. He had played with snakes back home and this one looks plenty fun. The snake coils. A rattling sounds catches his curiosity. "Lookie there," he reaches to touch the swinging tail. A blur of rock, dust, and snake erupts in front of the boy, and he fumbles to the ground.

"What the hell, boy." The toughest kid in Highland, Mississippi, uses a stick to send the rock-dazed snake into the woods. "Reachin fer a rattler. Sense of a goat, you got."

"Hiram, that Clay was the goofiest kid I ever did meet. He'd a ben dead more than once ifn I hadn't been around. Almost died on one occasion."

Alex tells the story of the night Frank saved Clay from

Mr. Miller's knife.

"It took him two days before he got himself out his dismals. He got out of it sure, and back to his goofy self." Alex pauses then repeats, "He always got himself out of his dismals."

Hiram processes what he just heard. Hiram knows the dismals Alex talks about. He too has seen that vacant stare in Clay, whenever life treats him unfairly. Like when a professor told Clay he wasn't fit for college. For two days Clay moved around in a dark silence. On the third day, Clay read a line Emerson, 'Nothing is at last sacred but the integrity of your own.' Clay recited it to himself until the light in him returned.

"Like a flower searching out the sun." Hiram now realizes what he likes the most about Clay.

Yeah, that's it, Hiram. But this is diffrnt."

"I respectfully disagree, Alex," Hiram responds. "He'll be stronger for it."

"Na, that old nigger was all he had. His Ma disappeared into herself not too long into her marriage to the old man. Her dyin was just dyin. She was dead long before. Frank was all Clay had, and now he's gone. Clay ain't comin back from this one."

"No, Alex. Clay has himself. He has himself, and that's all he'll ever need. He'll be stronger than ever."

Chapter Ten

December 24th, 1862

From the captain's tent, the Hogg Mess sprints like they've been let out of school. Opening Clay's tent, they gang pull the covers from him.

"Get up," they call in unintentional unison.

Clay turns over putting his jacket over his head.

"You need to get up. We have something for you." Rut pulls a piece of paper from his jacket pocket then pulls the jacket from Clay's face.

"Great, you got a pass to town," Clay speaks in the monotone of a man wanting to be left alone.

"Rut, you imbecile," Alex chortles. Rut switches papers.

"I have a day pass to town?" Clay questions.

"Compliments of the captain," Alex butts in. "Says he can't stand the sight of a soldier sulking like a girl. Said he doesn't trust ya'll to go and find fun for yourself, so he's sendin us along."

George Stewart pipes in, "We need to be back by noon tomorrow."

Too empty to fight, Clay mechanically joins the group on their trek to Murfreesboro, Tennessee. Leading the pack, Alex and Tucker poke at each other and foretell of the hell they'll raise. Hiram and Rut walk side by side. Needham Braird and George Stewart walk slightly behind. Clay drags tail.

Murfreesboro, a Tennessee town south of Nashville, once quiet, now finds itself on the road net of war; Bragg's army chokes the streets with wagons and men look for diversion. The Hogg Mess arrives to local citizens scurrying to avoid soldier's approaches, their civilian shoes stepping in army mule droppings; ladies shield themselves with lavender-doused napkins while menfolk vigilantly guard their women from the stares of soldiers long devoid of soft company. Night has brought out hurricane lamps and torches. Standing at the intersection of two congested roads, the Mess takes in the chaos.

"I could use some shoes," Rut offers an idea. Clay looks down at his shoes. Tired before he joined the army, they are tattered from the miles he's travelled since leaving Highland, yet he thinks he can still see hints of the shit from the Miller Farm stained in the leather.

Needham Braird, the oldest and worldliest, gets it moving, "The railhead. Better action there." The rest follow.

As the Hogg Mess passes a torch lit street corner, they come across a table bearing sweets and Christian inspiration. A herd of soldiers crowds the table; not so much for the epicurean invitation, but for the female attendants. Three fresh belles of the South offer food and drink to the war weary soldiers of Bragg's army.

Alex smells the game, "Come on, fellas." He clears a path for his comrades.

Christians by training, yet temptresses of the age when women know their power over men, the three go without shawls, shivering like ladies, flaunting coquettish smiles. Alex shoves Clay to the front. The prettiest one retreats a step. Tightness grows in Clay's stomach as he stares at the smallness of her waist.

"Where ya from?" the homeliest uses flirtation to draw in what beauty does for others.

"Tennessee. Arkansas…" men yip.

"And you?" she says to Clay.

Clay retreats a step. Hiram laughs. Alex pushes Clay back to the front.

The pretty one has moved on to an Alabama officer while the comely one smiles at Clay. A spark grows in him. Clay remembers a poem Hiram taught him.

"Who gave thee, O Beauty? The keys of this breast…" The word 'breast' allows her to use her well-practiced blushing.

Only Hiram knows the source of the line, one studied in college, and he winks in approval. Clay smiles, his mind plays and his body begins to awaken. With gossamer touch, she slides her fingers slowly down his; pausing just before the end. She makes sure her fingers send an electric shock through Clay's body. She leaves a cookie in his hand

and an urge in his private reaches. The world blurs. He feels warm inside. His eyes rip at the calico covering her full bosom.

With practiced timing that makes her popular, but not scandalous, the coquette moves to Alex. Before Clay has a chance to retreat into himself again, Needham comes up,

"Why look at candy when you can eat some?" he spits a wad of tobacco juice. "Come with me, boy. See ifn we can get us some real refreshment." Taking Clay by the elbow, they quickly head to the unpainted side of town, leaving the rest to eat sweet treats. "Want a pull?" Needham offers his canteen.

Dry mouthed, Clay prepares for a hearty swig of water. Throwing back the canteen, his chapped lips foretell the burning of local whiskey plunging down his unsuspecting throat. He nearly gags under its intensity. This first taste of liquor has his eyes watering and his chest fighting for air.

"Life will do that to ya. Expect one thing, get another." Needham says as he takes a man-size pull. Clay turns down a second chance. "Here we is." Needham turns to Clay in a father-to-son tone. "Assumin yer just as fresh with woman as ya'll ar with liquar, pay heed."

Needham's well-worn features tell of a man who has lived rough most of his life. Clay watches intently as Needham points to an unpainted shack, more of a shed than a house, where three doors partner with three windows, two of them haphazardly boarded up, no doubt broken in a drunken row, glow candlelight for the occupants.

"See there, boy, them windows that's lit. That means the gal inside's riding the bull. A dark window with the candle by the door means the girl needs more."

Clay follows Needham to a handrail set up to protect the girls from pro-bono requests. On the porch, a bear of a man sits, cudgel on his lap.

"Follow my lead," Needham steps up.

"Gotta knife or pocket pistol on ya?" Big Bob snaps.

Grabbing his crotch, Needham says, "I got a bayonet."

Big Bob's meaty hands grab ass and limb in search of derringers or Arkansas Toothpicks. Roughly handled, Needham ignores the assault, knowing the man is protecting the girls from men who find excitement in killing a whore. Cleared of weapons, Needham begins to move past the handrail when a drunken cavalry sergeant brings a candle to a door. Clay's not ready for this. The idea of being intimate challenges the protective wall he's built around himself. Fear locks the door. Clay begins to retreat. Needham keeps him moving forward.

"Two choices, welp. Step up or step out," Big Bob roars.

Before Clay can think, the man next in line shoves him forward. After the same brutal invasion of man-hands, Clay passes the guard rail to where Needham waits outside the middle door, one hand on the door handle, one hand on the candle. He offers his next piece of advice: "Now, boy, the first thing ya do is backhand her. That'll establish the relationship," he winks. "Make her more eager ta please," he says and enters the room.

A moment later Clay hears a slap and a thud. Clay always imagined his first time with a woman more like the feeling of Julie's voice reading a Blake poem, not the crass sounds, musky smells, and a well-travelled candle. He thinks back to that summer with Julie when he imagined himself caressing her skin, his lips moving from her neck to the sweet taste of her lips. That's what Clay wanted from his first time—the tightness in his stomach released into her as angels sang loves songs. The thought of a bruised whore shrinks his manhood.

"Get in or get the hell out of the way," Big Bob's voice sends Clay for the candle just brought out by another cavalry sergeant.

"Left you some," he laughs. Clay enters the small space, the musky smell of sex and sweat lie thick in the air. The candle provides the only light.

"Hey, sugar," comes a soft voice in the darkness. "Be with ya in a moment. Just gotta clean myself up."

From behind a blind set in the corner of the room, he hears the sound of water rung from a cloth.

"Have a sit on the bed."

In a room barely large enough for a bed and a small end table, he does as he's told. Placing the candle on the bed stand near the window, he notices a half empty bottle of laudanum and an ambrotype of a soldier. The soldier is about the same age as Clay, but confident of posture. On his uniformed lap sits a baby, and next to him a wife holding the baby's hand. Clay finds the woman handsome, and hopes the sound behind the blind comes from the woman in the image. For every soldier killed, an orphan is born. For every husband slain, a prostitute is born. In the next room Clay hears Needham slaps a dead man's wife. Love and life are nothing like what Clay imagined.

"Thought you'd be undressed by now."

From behind the blind stands a withered vine of youth. The woman from the image, but her face has long lost itself in hard lines, worn down by the weight of a life chosen for her by war.

"Best hurry before we're not alone. Big Bob don't like wasted time."

She pulls her dress over her head exposing articulated ribs emptying into a scarred stomach and deep scratches from earlier patrons. She approaches. The girl at the church had ample breasts and a light touch. This one's boyish chest does nothing to ignite a passion unquenched. She gets to work, her skilled fingers working the brass buttons of his uniform jacket, and before he knows it, Clay stands a button away from being naked in front of a woman. She slides down his pants where he watches her head move piston like. Clay begins to grow. Pulling her head back, she examines his excitement and smiles in approval. His mind shuts off. Her touch charges his entire body.

In a whoosh, she pulls him onto the bed. His pants at his ankles, he loses his balance and falls on her, and she lets out a painful groan as his full weight lands on her. Recovering her breath, her hand moves down to stroke him. The stimulation is too much for a boy who has never felt a woman. Before he starts, he's finished.

"That's okay, sugar. I like it when boys like me that much." She begins to pull herself away when she notices something, "Looks like you're still game," she smiles.

Clay enters a world where the carnal actions supplant conscious thought. At first Clay thinks, and wonders, and fears while he tries to find where he's supposed to go. She winces as his erection hits everywhere but. Clay begins to grow scared. *What am I doing wrong?* He begins to lose it when a soft hand guides him in. Then she quiets his brain with one single phrase.

"Take me."

Oh yes.

Clay becomes a closed-eyed piston of spasmodic energy driving and pumping without thought. Sweat drips from his forehead into her squinting eyes. All too quickly, his back arches and his eyes roll back. He finishes. Taking a long breath, Clay opens his eyes to her green eyes looking into him. And he looks into her. In her eyes, he sees all the potential of the world, all the potential of himself. The physical becomes spiritual. Their noses touch as he begins the slow rhythm of lovemaking. Her hips mold into his. Clay becomes the moment. She squeezes him tight. Their eyes make love; their bodies become one in rhythmic simplicity. They finish.

"Put the candle out by the door when you leave sugar." She says as she glides to behind the blind. Clay put his pants on to the sound of water and scrubbing. He dresses too slowly, wanting more of everything he just experienced.

Coming out from behind the curtain, "You still here, sugar," she says. Her eyes will not look at Clay. "If you wanna go again, goin to hafta get back in line." Clay tries to get into her eyes again, but she won't look at him. He grows cold again.

Clay Miller pays for the service then leaves. Placing the candle in the doorway, he looks onto a crass world of men waiting to release their carnal urges. As soon as he puts the candle by the door, an artillery crew charges en mass. Shoving each man as they pass, Clay makes them pay for what they are about to do. They could have fought the boy, but why when a whore awaits. The last cannon cock slams her door behind him. Her candle light glows.

Needham comes up and offers a pull. Clay takes it in gulps. "Are you in love?"

"Not sure."

Clay thinks of the light of her emerald eyes. "She only charged me for two of the three since the first one was so quick."

"That does it, you melted the heart of a whore," Needham laughs as he offers another pull from his canteen, "Merry Christmas."

The two spend the rest of the night under the railway station awning draining the canteen. From where they sit, they can see the whores at work; their candles moving from door to window and back in a continuous rhythm.

Between swigs, Clay ponders this night of firsts; alcohol numbs the mind and deafens the senses, making cold the emptiness in him. Yet, his moment of intimacy has somehow softened his heart just a bit. In silence, both men pass the canteen until sleep overtakes them.

Chapter Eleven

December 25th, 1862

Awakening, the headache of a first drunk pierces Clay's head. His brain burns. Last night, Clay found the alcohol a balm, now he swears it off like a temperance rally convert.

Needing water, Clay leaves a snoring Needham to search for relief. Bundling himself the best he can, he passes the darkened sheds of sleeping whores when he spots the chair that Big Bob squatted on. A swift kick and the chair lands half submerged in a puddle of mud.

Head throbbing, he comes around the corner where he sees the table from last night is still manned, but this time by the older Christian variety.

"Good morning, soldier. My, you are an early riser."

"Yes, ma'am."

"Are you heading to church on this most holy day?"

Steaming cups of chicory and soggy molasses cookies call to him.

"Son," the most matronly moves toward Clay. "Have you dedicated your life to Jesus?

A pregnant pause, "No, ma'am." Clay walks away; hypocrisy wouldn't go well with chicory and cookies.

Arriving at a nearby well, he begins to fill his canteen when he hears,

"Hey, Clay, where did you head off to?" It's Alex.

"Clay," Hiram half embraces him. "Did you find some better lines of poetry?"

"Horizontal Emerson," Clay offers.

"Good choice," Hiram smiles like he understands.

For the next five minutes Clay hears about their evening's adventures. Alex and the rest found a warm church to sleep in. When they find out Clay spent the night with Needham, they offer their condolences for having to be with such a brute. "Not so bad," is all Clay will give.

Stewart breaks the reunion, "Hey, boys, we best be heading back. Our pass is only good til noon today."

Beginning their walk under blue skies, they pass men heading away from camp and those, like themselves, hurrying to return. One can tell the temperature of the day by the stance of a soldier; cold days have shoulders pulled up by the ears and hands in the pockets, while warm days have top buttons undone and hands swaying in counter rhythm to legs. Clay walks the walk of a cold man on a warm day.

Between the camp and the town, they come upon a grey-faced farmstead where the army provost has set up a military jail; the outbuildings quartering the provost guard and the corral housing the reprobates and shirkers that left the deviancy of life back home to be the same kind of men in the army. Drunken men like Needham have spent time there along with the cowards, nar-do-wells, and even the innocent. Next to the farm house a throng of citizens and soldiers create a commotion that draws the Hogg Mess toward it. Moving closer to the commotion they stop near a hitched wagon where Clay's hangover has him leaning against the tailgate.

"Hey, mister, what's with this?" Alex asks an old gentleman.

"It would appear Bragg has caught himself a spy. He means to make a public statement with him."

"Spy?"

"That detestable Yankee, General Rosecrans has spies everywhere. Bragg can't have supper without that Yankee general knowing what's for dessert. It would appear this one got a bit too close to the fire," the old man says before he makes his way to the front of the crowd. "Gonna to be a hanging."

From the door, Clay sees the provost marshal step out with another man in tow. Hands shackled, dressed in a fine silk vest and broadcloth black pants, he stands on excellent boots. Although well-manicured, he needs a shave. In spite of the cold, he stands erect while Clay shivers.

"Move aside," the provost marshal orders the crowd as he pushes his charge to the back of the wagon where Clay gets a close look at the spy. Immediately he sees the same grace borne from breeding he sees in Hiram. Erect but not haughty, the sharp eyes and the closed mouth of a thinker.

A curiosity awakens as Clay watches a man about to meet the noose standing like a man in control of himself. He stops next to Clay.

"You there," barks the provost. "Help the spy into the wagon."

Clay notices something shiny on the spy's lapel; a gold pin, about two inches long, in the shape of an axe. The axe reminds Clay of his loss. Frank.

"You there. Get that man into the wagon!" The provost booms.

Clay's eyes fix on the pin and the memories of happy times in the woods with Frank.

"You like it?" the spy notices Clay's focus.

"Where did you get that?" Clay wants one. He wants to keep those memories alive.

Smiling, the spy replies, "Well, if you had voted for Lincoln, you could have had one. Then again," the spy takes a slow look around, "you'd be in the same fix I am."

Highland was not a Lincoln town, nor was Mississippi for that matter. Clay only liked him because people called him 'The Railsplitter.' but he didn't vote for him, or even vote. The pin makes him wish he had.

Just then Clay feels a shove that drives him into the spy. Turning, he sees the provost's reddened face, "Damn you. I said throw this piece of dung into the wagon so we can get to hanging him."

The spy turns to Clay, "Do you mind giving me a hand?"

Maybe to escape the thoughts of Frank. Maybe because

there is something to this man and his story, Clay accepts the offer to help.

"Her too," barks the provost.

Turning, Clay sees of a woman in her early thirties and beautiful in the way he always dreamed of a woman; slender, shapely with brown hair and green eyes. Last night's urge rekindles.

The spy's voice interrupts, "This is my wife. It would be surely appreciated if you might help her up so we may have one more ride together."

One hand on her wrist, the other around the small of her waist, his mind goes places inappropriate for the moment. Just as quickly, a voice inside punishes him for being so crass. Casting his eyes away, Clay moves back from the wagon.

"Jump in, private. I'll need your help when we get to the gallows," orders the provost. Alex and the rest of the mess watch as Clay rides toward a large oak tree sitting in the middle of a field not far from the house. From it a hangman's rope hangs limp. Alex waves as they head back to camp.

For the next few moments Clay sits on one side of the wagon while a husband and a wife desperately try to share a moment. Embarrassed for his earlier carnal thought and unused to seeing genuine love, Clay stares at the muddy ruts that follow the wagon's movement while gentle whispers sneak past the wagon's creaks and groans. Sobbing punctuates hushed love. The wagon hits a rut sending the spy and his wife into Clay where he feels the woman against his chest. Just as quickly, he properly helps her back to her spot. Clay's noble act rekindles pride in himself.

"Thank you," she says politely.

They arrive at an aged oak tree, the wagon stopping almost directly under a horizontal branch stout enough to hold a dead man's weight.

"Get her off the wagon," the provost orders Clay.

Hoping off, he looks at the woman, seeing in her a resignation of her future, and he assumes a hate for her husband's choices, as well as a pride in her husband's honor. She is alive in her love of him. Clay wonders if someone will feel the same about him when her graceful slide to earth brings Clay back to the world.

Clay's mind now attaches itself to the actions of the spy. Some men live life by a clear navigation point. Clay's entire life has been buffeted by the wind and weather of life, with neither a star nor compass to set his course by. The spy appears to have set his course by a single-minded purpose—to be a man of ideals. The fact he spied for Lincoln shows conviction to an ideal, and his demeanor as he is before the noose shows he sees value in himself. He stands tall with his decision, accepting the price of his actions. *No wonder his wife loves him*, Clay thinks.

"Now get that Lincolnite off the wagon," snarls the provost as if he's the moral compass of the Confederacy.

Polished boots drop to earth. The weight of the moment buckles the spy for just a moment, a moment Clay races to.

"Let the coward stand for himself," the provost commands.

"I'm alright," taking a deep breath, the spy collects himself.

Clay remembers watching Frank during the time when he had one foot in the light and one foot on earth. He saw the regality of a good man continue through the last. He stood tall just like this spy. Clay sees the man he wants to be.

Moving next to her husband, the woman whispers, "Be strong."

Their hands intertwined, their eyes lock in each other one last moment before the rope tightens. The moment comes. The life ends. If dying well is important, then he died well. Frank did as well. They both died with their dignity intact.

Spectacle over, just Clay, the officiates, the old man from the provost building, and the wife are left when Clay is ordered to load the deadweight into the wagon where his wife waits for her husband. Tears falling, she caresses her husband's hair in a tender moment meant for them alone. Clay begins to retreat from the wagon. She looks up.

"My husband wanted you to have this," the widow hands Clay the golden axe from her husband's lapel. The wagon pulls away.

The old man from town comes up, "He died well. No one can ever take that from him."

Clay puts the pin on his jacket.

Chapter Twelve

Leaving the sound of a wagon rolling away, Clay moves toward the camp in the tired gait of a man who has learned a lot for one day. Coming upon the outskirts of camp, Clay sees a line of men waiting at the road guard while the officer of the day, his crimson sash worn over his shoulder like a blanket roll, checks each man's pass. Clay also sees The Hogg Mess nervously waiting in line. He slides in behind Rut.

"Now what?" Clay asks.

"We're three hours late. Maybe we should take to the woods," Alex says nervously.

Rut offers his two-bits, "Na, let's go straight in. Three hours ain't nothin. Sides, take us longer if we go through the woods. Be that much later."

The group walks up to the officer and offer their passes. Being late might get the boys a ride on the wooden horse, or maybe a knapsack full of rocks. Not deadly, but not pleasant either.

Rut whispers to Alex, "This doesn't look good. Going to be punished for sure." Alex speaks from experience, "I don't want to ride the wooden horse again. Nearly busted my balls last time."

Clay remembers Alex sitting on the wooden horse for back talking an officer back in Pensacola. For two hours Alex sat on a horizontal log the length of a horse with firewood-sized logs tied to his ankles to increase the weight, and to top it off he had to carry a big wooden sword as added weight and pain.

"They could hang us," Clay says, his mind seeing the swinging spy.

Rut becomes attracted to the shiny object on Clay's chest, "Wher'd ya get that pin?"

Before Clay can respond, Stewart stops the silliness, "Okay, settle down, they don't execute men for being late."

"Only spies die on Christmas," Clay offers a statement more for himself than others.

The officer returns, "Why are you boys so late?"

Hiram steps up, "Sir, my companion, Clay that is, well, he has been lost in melancholy. We thought some time in town would act like the balm of Gilead. Our mission of tending to a crestfallen soldier stole our appreciation for time."

"Poetic, but a bit farcical." The lieutenant flexes his own education. "Did your fallen hero arise again?"

"Phoenix-like, sir," Hiram enjoys the word play.

"Well, do you feel cheered up?" the officer turns to Clay.

Clay's mind runs through the events of the last twenty-four hours, "As much as a man can be, sir." The boys are free.

Just as the officer returns the passes, General Braxton Bragg and his minions ride up. Aides and staff along with Clay's division commander ride next to General Breckenridge, former vice president, and a Kentuckian. Bragg halts his procession.

"What's the meaning of this, Lieutenant?" he glares down at the officer.

With a salute the lieutenant begins, "General, some men late from leave. Just about to scold them then send them on their way."

Steam spews from Bragg as he hears the words 'on their way' and says, "Damn if you will. Arrest these men."

"Going to have them shot too," Breckinridge's sarcasm is palpable.

The lieutenant defends the boys, "Sir, they're only a bit late."

Bragg doesn't hear the junior officer, preferring a larger target. He turns to Breckinridge, "You Kentuckians are too independent for the good of the army. I'll shoot every one of them if I have to."

"We ain't Kentuckians," Alex barks.

Bragg ignores Alex to continue his tirade on the Kentucky general, "General Breckinridge, desertion and shirking of any kind will break down the morale of this army, and I, sir, will not have it." He turns back to the lieutenant, "Arrest these men and put them with the two condemned men." Then Bragg notices the brassy glint of Clay's pin. "Lieutenant, that man. The one with the shiny object on his jacket. Bring him to me."

The lieutenant, his face tight and his eyes on fire, looks past his antagonist, "Yes, sir."

A firm hand pushes Clay toward General Bragg, the most powerful man Clay has ever seen, larger and more imposing than Mr. Miller ever was. Clay stumbles to catch his breath, and his fear of powerful men floods to the forefront.

"What's that pin, boy?" Bragg questions.

Clay balks at the question, afraid to answer like a child's fear of answering a question that brings trouble.

"Are you a Lincoln man, private?" Before he has time to respond, "Are you a spy?" Bragg questions.

Like a child, he answers the simple truth. "I like axes."

"We'll see what you are," Bragg's intense face and tight-lipped words become knife threatening. "Lieutenant, place that man under arrest." Bragg looks to Clay's mess. "Them too."

"Yes, Sir."

As Bragg is about to leave, he laughs sardonically, "Tomorrow is a good day for a firing squad."

"We'll be shot fer sur," Rut exclaims.

"Shut up, Rut." Stewart quiets the fear.

The mess finds itself put into a hog pen next to the provost building.

As the provost closes the gate, he turns to Stewart. "You

boys will be in a firin squad tomorra." He points to two men in gray uniforms huddled by the fire in the middle of the pen. "Deserters. Kind of like you except them were caught whereas you turned yourself in."

Before Stewart can challenge the corporal's semantics, the rest of the boys leave him for the furthest corner from the prisoners. Stewart joins their tight pack. Alex stares silently at the two men. Hiram studies them as well. Not Clay however. The confinement of the hog pen is beginning to grate on him. Like a cat caught in the corner, Clay wants to get away, but isn't sure how. Backing up to the fence, he turns his head toward the hanging tree not so far away, where an empty rope still swings in the breeze. The image of the spy's bulging eyes and protruding tongue turns him back to the hog pen where he sees one of the prisoners stand up for a slow, pained stretch and then returns to his crouch.

"Too cold to stand back here when there's a perfectly good fire yonder," Rut says, breaking the silence. Ignoring the tension, he moves toward the two men. "Is this fire for dead men only?"

Hiram gasps. Alex laughs, and the rest wait to see how the condemned will react to Rut. Clay watches too. Rut is the kind of man who will say anything to get a reaction, often to the dismay of those around him. One never knows what'll come out of his mouth. Still, there is an honesty in what he says, and a purity in what he does. One of the condemmed men rises. Alex moves in followed by the rest.

Tension stands up when Rut does his thing.

"You can call me Rut."

Alex jumps in, "You can call him mule ass if you prefer."

The golden light of the roaring campfire illuminates the standing prisoner. Shadows darken the features of his face, yet the light offers just enough to see his gaped teeth appear in a smile. Tension sits down.

"We do," Alex finishes.

Clay, for a moment, leaves his inner world to see Rut act the way he does to make others happy. *Good man*. Rut introduces each of the mess, and in turn, the condemned introduce themselves.

"Asa Lewis, 6th Kentucky of the Orphan Brigade," offers the one who looks like a farmer, who stood up earlier.

"Percy Willick, 60th North Carolina," offers the one with The Book in his hand.

For the awkward moment that follows introductions, the seven men warm themselves with the fire. Percy Willick returns to his testament. Asa notices the gold pin on Clay's chest.

"You a Lincoln man? I'm going to be shot by a Lincoln man." Asa fires. "Well, don't that beat all?"

Alex too is curious about the pin, "Yea, Clay, where did you get that? You ain't no Lincoln lover."

Recalling the hanging makes Clay shudder, "Got it off that dead Yankee spy." He pauses. "Really, I just like axes."

Hiram tells Clay the origin of the pin. "The Railsplitter. Lincoln used it as a campaign ribbon."

Clay says, "It's just an ax."

"No, Clay, it's more than that and trouble will follow it," Alex reminds his friend.

Asa Lewis changes the timbre of the corral, "Are Mississippi boys good shots?"

Rut proudly announces, "Hell yeah, boy. Best in the army."

"Shut up, Rut," Alex stops him from making it worse.

Before long, Stewart, Rut, Alex and the rest go to sleep in a huddled pile. Their blankets are back at camp. Only the Kentuckian, the North Carolinian and one Mississippian remain by the fire, the three absorbed in the hypnotic dance of the flames. The North Carolinian fixates on the smoke disappearing into the night sky while the Kentuckian stares intently at the embers. Clay rubs his pin wishing he were back at the woodlot with Frank. The brass handle brings back the feeling of Old Thunder and the smell that follows a good strike of the axe against a tree fills his mind. The thwack of the imagined strike resonates over the sounds of the guards talking outside the corral.

"What's ya doin there, Mississippi?"

Clay continues caressing the golden axe handle.

"Said, what ya doin?"

Clay's hand drops. In the near distance Rut's snoring draws a kick from someone in the sleeping pile. Clay looks up. "Why are you here, Kentucky?"

"Asa Lewis."

"Asa Lewis, from Kentucky, why are you here?" Clay knows why the spy died, but why this man? His jacket sleeve shows he was once a corporal.

North Carolina lets out a perceptible sigh. Kentucky takes a deep breath then confesses. "Pa died, Ma needed help bringing the crops in so I lit out for home. Unfortunately, they got me before I could hang a hog."

"Why didn't you ask for a furlough?"

"Tried and was denied, so I left. Had every intention of coming back once the hogs was slaughtered, ham smoked, and sausage made. Bounty hunter got me two miles from camp."

Like a cold wind, the idea of a man being shot for trying to help bring in the harvest slaps Clay. *That just doesn't wash. Of all the possible punishments, why a firing squad?*

"I was promoted to 4th corporal for bravery at Shiloh," Asa semi-proudly states.

Most officers are fairly sympathetic to a private's plight, coming from the same orchard as their men. *What general could ever do something this draconian, as Hiram would say?* Clay ponders.

"Did Bragg have anything to do with your sentence?" *Clay touches the pin as if protecting it from Bragg's glare.*

Asa's eyes attack the question. "Yes, sir, he did. After I was turned down, I asked fer an audience with Braxton Bragg hisself. I asked him, 'General' I said, 'I served honorably at Shiloh and intend to see this conflict through.

If you could see fit to let me get home and tend to the farm, I promise to be back by the New Year.' Well, he looks at me, examinin me like I'm a piece of putrid salt pork, then he said these words. He said, 'Your duty is to the army first—above God and family.' Can ya imagin, above God and family?" *Bragg's as bad as Mr. Miller.* "That son of a bitch only cares about meat for the grinder. Soldier's ain't nothing but forage to be eaten by the war then shit out in graves all across the South." He begins to sob. "Guess I'll be shit out in Tennessee."

North Carolina cries in his fetal position, Asa Lewis, from Kentucky, sobs over his fate and, Clay Miller, from Mississippi, waits for the dawn.

"Mississippi, are you a good shot?"

December 26ᵗʰ, 1862

A diagonal rain pounds the chilled bodies of the two groups of men.

"Not a few hundred yards from here, we got us a nice cabin half built and here we are freezin our asses off thanks to the jackass with the gold braid and grey beard," Alex complains about Bragg.

Asa Lewis rises as best he can, "Well, at least ya'll sleep warm and dry tonight. I'll be just startin ta rot."

Someone always has it worse, and in that Clay appreciates the significance of what Asa says. Stoic. Pragmatic. True. A staff officer with two Negroes comes near, each Negro carrying a last supper for the condemned. Nothing for the shooters. North Carolina drinks the coffee first seemingly disinterested in the corn mush and bacon on his plate. Clay sees Alex eyeing the bacon on North Carolina's plate. They all stare at the plate. Even Stewart wipes the drool from the corner of his lips. Hunger trumps civility.

"Ifn you ain't hungry, I'll volunteer for that duty," Alex slides closer.

North Carolina's nod sends Alex diving for the rashers of bacon. Hiram spoons the mush and the rest fight for what's available. Rut licks the remaining mush from the plate. Clay stands still not sure to quench his hunger or stand on a principle that's being violated in front of him. He silently passes on the mush and bacon.

While his pards devour a man's last meal, Clay looks to Asa. Last night the flicker of life shone in him, but today the color has left his face, and his body trembles like Frank's did. In spite of the rain that slaps at his face and the cold wind blowing, Asa's shaking seems internally born. His cup of coffee cools by his feet and his bacon goes cold. Clay moves toward him.

"Hungry?" Asa asks.

The stomach says yes, but he answers, "Not really."

"Are you in your letters, there Mississippi?"

In a flush of enthusiasm for what Clay interprets as someone recognizing he has value, his mind prepares to tell Asa Lewis about his brief college career, his love of

Emerson, his time spent with Julie reading the classics, but he stops. His moments seem rather small in this moment. "Yes."

"If I give ya'll a task, would ya parform it?"

"Sure."

"Na, ain't good nuff. I need your salum vow. Will ya parform it?"

Clay takes a deep breath. "I will."

"Good." He then tells Clay to write his mother with the news of his death, and where to get his body.

"Tell 'em, I tried to git home. Tell 'em all that they were in my heart to the last." His face tightens. "I ain't no coward, so make sure they knows it. Ain't shot fer that." He turns to his bacon and coffee.

Sergeant Major Dix, promoted after Perryville, walks up with nine men, including Needham, carrying their muskets and one for each of the Hogg Mess.

Asa shudders at the sight of the cold steel barrels. North Carolinian offers a near silent, "Oh God."

"Firing Squad, fall in one rank by height," Dix orders.

A firing squad is murder with military window dressing, and since soldiers aren't supposed to murder, the army sets up firing squads so men can dignify their participation and excuse their actions. Half of the muskets will carry lead, and the other half will not. That way a man can question whether his musket did the deed or not.

For reasons only known to Bragg, he's not having men of the condemned's regiments do the killing, so the 7th

Mississippi detail marches across a rain swept field to
the open end of a hollow square of men made up of the
Kentucky brigade on one side and the North Carolina
brigade on the other. Shivering hundreds have been
ordered to witness Bragg's discipline on their own.

"Detail, Halt. Front." The squad halts just ahead of
Bragg and his horsed staff.

Twenty yards in front of them, two man-height posts
have been driven into the ground. Tied to the left post,
North Carolina more hangs than stands as he cries for
his savior to save him. North Carolina's last moments on
earth pale when compared to the spies.

On the right post, Asa Lewis tilts his face to the rain.
Opening his mouth, he tastes each drop, then, in a moment
of calm, lowers his head to see the Mississippi men.

Suddenly a commotion occurs to the right, "Skunk!"
A North Carolina company retreats from the upturned
tail. Laughter and commotion ruin the solemnity of the
moment, bringing Bragg to a boil. Asa lets out a karmic
laugh. North Carolina hasn't noticed. A sword through
the body ends the skunk's reign. Back to business.

A staff officer fights the wind and rain to read the
orders of execution. North Carolina continues to weep.
Asa locks eyes on Clay, digging deep into him for that
human connection of souls, wanting a word or a nod,
something that says, it will be okay, you'll be missed, you
have value. Anything to prove someone cares. Clay feels
those eyes digging into a dark recess Clay himself hasn't

explored. He averts his eyes. He fails. He fails because he can't give what he's just now aware of. He can't. Not yet. He tilts his head to the ground as the orders are finished.

The staff officer now asks each man if he has any last words. North Carolina cries out, "Take me, lord."

Asa gives his last words, "Clay Miller." Clay looks up. "Aim to kill."

General Bragg rides up to give instructions to the firing squad when he sees the pin on Clay's jacket.

In a rage, "What is the meaning of this? Get that damnable Lincoln loving radical out of this formation before I have him join those two."

Instantly, Sergeant Major Dix sprints towards Clay, and with a quick shove, has him out of the firing squad and near General Breckinridge.

"Ready."

Muskets drawn to the diagonal. Hammers put to half cock.

"Aim!"

Muskets to shoulders—full cock.

"FIRE!"

The musket smoke quickly blows away exposing the North Carolinian writhing about; two red spots grow, one near his left knee and the other mid stomach. The Kentuckian lies motionless, his neck pulsating a diminishing stream of blood. Each pulse shortens until it stops. He's dead. The staff officer walks to the North Carolinian and, pulling his navy colt from the holster, administers the final shot.

The wind grows colder. The rain begins to freeze and Clay goes back to camp to write a letter that will go nowhere. Asa hadn't told Clay where he was from. Clay takes the pin off and hides it in the same poke sack that hides Transcendentalism.

Chapter Thirteen

News Year Eve, 1862

The Cowen House, brick and mortar, laying in heaps about the edges of a once manicured plantation home has met the destructive force of two armies this day. Thin trails of smoke from its timbers rise into a leaden sky filled with the sounds of picket fire. Freezing rain bites at his exposed skin. Clay's shoes have run out of miles, further shredded in today's attack across the cotton field. They are more exposed skin than leather binding. The moisture of the day has soaked his socks. Each step to the potential safety of the house soaks his feet even more. About him thousands of confederates lie wrecked, their moans and screams echoing across the cotton field recently defended by the battered but vigilant Federal Army of General Rosecrans. Hiding behind buildings or even the rows of a farm field, the survivors of the day's attack inspect themselves for damage. Using the remains of the house for protection from Yankee lead, Clay lays his musket down for the first time since dawn. The explosion of sixty rounds heated the barrel to the point of burning Clay's fingers. Now cooled, the musket sits on a pile of bricks torn from the chimney by union artillery fire. Picking up an undamaged brick, he can feel the heat of the earlier fire still alive in it. Now he cools like the brick does, the fire of battle leaving his body. He finds his jacket and pants perforated by three bullet holes too close to meat to ponder. Clay reflects on the last day of 1862.

He inspects the bricks as if they were individuals. He picks up one without blemish or mark: George Stewart was the last to retreat; standing alone, he fired his musket at the Yankees with deliberate precision. God makes so few good men and he wanted Stewart to last a bit longer. It's painful to admit, but Julie married well. He picks up a brick as cold as Asa Lewis. The broken pieces of the chimney remind Clay of the broken pieces of his company. He saw James Thornhill burst into a red mist as a cannon ball went through him and George Wharton. Wharton flopped about like a newly caught fish. Each brick represents a comrade fallen: Jonathon Sermons, Will Johnston, and Lieutenant Harrigill. He finds one broken into four pieces, one ragged piece for each child Rut left behind. Clay will never forget the joy of seeing Rut play with his children. The laughter of the boys will be forever replaced with sight of Rut falling. Charred beams, smashed window panes, collapsed walls—these shattered bricks and lives sum up 1862.

The last battle of year started out with two nights and

days of the 7th hidden behind a shallow trench scraped out by bare hands, bayonets, and plates in topsoil that barely covered bedrock. The night before, Bragg had ordered no fires so his men literally froze to the ground. Meanwhile the Yankee general built fires far beyond the length of their line so as to fool an enemy, already discovered, by making him think the Union line extended twice its actual length. In the morning Yankee General Rosecrans's ruse turned against him as Bragg attacked the very fires meant to ruse. The undefended area gave Bragg the exposed flank and he took it, pushing the Yankee right flank back almost onto itself. The roar of musketry filled the air as the battle moved closer and closer to where Clay and the boys from Highland waited their turn to attack. And attack they did. Two thousand Mississippians charged stiff limbed and frozen, but full of vigor past the Cowen House. General Chalmers looking gallant as he led the brigade on that first attack. The men cheered lustily as they struggled to keep the cadence. Then Yankee artillery had its fun, sending round shot bounding toward the 7th. That's how Thornhill and Wharton got it. Clay felt the whoosh of the cannon ball fly past him and through them both. Next the hell of case shot exploded over their heads, spraying iron rain onto men intent on looking forward. At one point an artillery shell took out three files—six men gone in less than a second. Their bodies still lie as they did when they died. Good regiments close ranks and continue. The officers ordered the survivors to close up. Wounded streamed to the rear, dead piled up, and still the regiment closed ranks and fired back in an ever-diminishing volume of defiance. A mangling wound ended General Chalmers' glory. Still the brigade continued. One hundred fifty yards to the blue line when Clay swore he heard a blue artillery officer call for canister. Cannons became shotguns spewing hundreds of pieces of grapeshot. More fell. Clay continued. Now less than eighty yards from the Yankees, a booming Blue voice gave a command heard across the battlefield. "Prepare to Fire!" Confederate ears strained to hear the next deadly command. "Aim!" Muskets leveled. "Fire" clearly heard just before the flash of thousands of Illinois, Kentucky, and Indiana muskets. A wall of lead raced toward Clay's brigade. Scores dropped as one. Scared? Foolish? Determined? Stupid? Yes, yes, yes, and YES! But that was earlier today. Tonight is about a different battle, just as dangerous.

Nightfall ended the battle and now the men, who hours before filled the skies with their yells, snore in frozen solitude around the Cowen House. Clay too begins to fall deep into sleep when he feels the whiz of a musket ball race just over his head. Another random shot is followed by two responding shots. Then all goes quiet. Awake now, Clay returns to the cold that has him shivering uncontrollably, attacking his feet as he curses the army for not providing shoes. He curses himself for joining the army. He even curses God once, then quickly takes it back.

Clear and brilliant, the stars shine frosty light on the

forms of men around him. He sees Hiram sleeping tight in his overcoat. On the other side of a smoldering beam, Tucker and Alex spoon. Putting his canteen to his chapped and bleeding lips, Clay gulps nothing. Damn it. A bullet has just punctured his canteen. He watches the last drops fall to earth. Clay flings the dead canteen against the wall.

"Hey, watch it," comes a voice upset by the sound of tin on brick.

Hunger is his never-ending tormenter, so Clay reaches into his haversack only to find a few crumbs and a thumb size piece of salt pork. Three days ago each man in the company received a pound and a half of salt pork and a handful of cornmeal. Since then, he's survived on that, a handful of parched corn stolen from the horse's feed, and two crackers Alex had squirreled away for the two of them. Starving and nearly barefoot, he won't last another night. He knows there are haversacks and shoes lying on the battlefield. A bullet sprints past Clay's head. Another Minnie ball clips the wall. No place to hide from death, he leaves the false security of the Cowen House to the slap of winter air. He looks across the battlefield then decides he better go as light as possible, just in case. He lays his musket, cartridge box, even his bayonet down next to Hiram. He may have to run for his life. He places his blanket on the sleeping friend. He decides his plan. He's not planning on going too close to the Yankee side of the field. He'll try the bodies closest to the house.

Following the path of the day's attack, he comes upon

a body half naked and missing his shoes. Next, a wounded man calls for his mother. In the half moon light, Clay sees other desperate men move from body to body checking pockets and haversacks. Clay wonders who's picking Rut's pocket. He comes to where the brigade went to ground, where its collective consciousness halted. Paper tails torn from musket rounds spit to the ground by men firing as fast as they could lie about in neat patterns, like snow, indicating when the battle line fired. Clay emptied his cartridge box here: forty rounds fired in haste at an enemy hidden behind clouds of smoke. A score of dead men lie in a neat row, as if on parade, killed by formation. Every one of them has been stripped of what Clay needs.

Thinking he sees a familiar hat, Clay kneels next to a shoeless body. He knows him. Crabtree, a cousin of the Currents, his jacket and shirt have been ripped open and his right index finger still plugs the hole in his stomach. His haversack is empty, but Clay takes the canteen. Survival is not a sentimentalist. A musket ball flies past.

The confederate dead have been stripped. *Now what?* Just a few rods ahead of him a confederate picket line holds fast, spaced out five paces between each man. Ahead of them will be a union counterpoint. His feet are beginning that cold burn just before frostbite. He may lose his toes unless he does something. No time for cowards, Clay decides to go where he knows haversacks are full and shoes abound. The union side of the field.

Silently sliding to the right just far enough behind the

picket line so as not be heard, he sees a patch of woods
to his front and right. The picket line has bent slightly,
leaving the woodlot unoccupied. At least he hopes. At the
edge of the wood he finds a crude barricade. Knowing that
only the Yankees were behind works this day, Clay knows
he is near enemy lines. Like a deer smelling a hunter, Clay
stands perfectly still. His eyes silently search for musket
barrels. His ears ache to hear anything except his own
racing heart. Taking a deep breath, he listens hard. His
feet force him forward slowly, quietly, his mind waiting
for the final bullet. He peers over the barricade of felled
timber and earth mounded chest high to find a dozen
dead federals. No living ones. Sucking in a deep breath of
relief, he awkwardly crawls over the barricade landing in
the middle of a full harvest of haversacks, intact shoes, and
heavy wool overcoats. Food is the first order of business
so he turns over the nearest Yankee whose face is gone
and a dark stain covers the entire front of his overcoat
and the strap to a heavy looking haversack. Not affected
by the sight, Clay pulls out his pocket knife and takes
the haversack from the body. Starvation greedily digs out
a soaked hard cracker and handful of wet coffee beans.
Ignoring the iron bite coating the coffee, he sucks the
marrow from the beans while chomping on the softened
hard tack. Savoring the moment, he baths in the flavors of
life. Surrounded by death, Clay lives.

Feeling energy again, Clay begins the search for shoes.
Moving to a dead sergeant sitting against the barricade

like he's taking a nap, Clay sits in front of him. He's glad the Yank's eyes are closed. He's had enough eyes for a while, and this is not the place he wants anyone looking into his soul. He has more base needs at this moment. He puts his right shoe to the Yank's to see if they are the same size. A smile explodes as Clay quickly pulls off his shoes and good riddance to their worn body and perforated soul, more than that, good bye to the last thing Clay has from Highland. In an energetic toss, they land on the other side of the barricade.

Removing the fresh Yankee shoes, he sees-Socks! Clay gently peels what appears to be brand new socks from the dead man's cold legs. He puts them on and the effect is immediate as thick wool embraces his feet, blanketing them in a warmth only wool can provide. Food in his stomach and his feet warming, Clay wiggles his toes in kid like play.

CLICK!

"Your lucky day, Reb. We just got issued shoes and socks the day before yesterday."

Clay takes a deep breath. His mind wonders if it will be his last, but when he should feel fear, he doesn't. He's not feeling the frozen reaction of his youth. He feels oddly calm. Not sure if it's the tone of the Yank or some interconnected voice telling him not to fear, he puts on his new shoes.

"Those shoes you tossed out had some miles to them."

Quietly, comfortably Clay rises, "They did. And I have

more miles to go," he responds matter-of-factly. Turning to the Yank, he offers his hand, "Clay Miller, 7th Mississippi Infantry."

CLICK, "Letting your guard down, if just for a minute, can get you killed." The Yankee, an officer, puts his pistol in its holster. "Bierce. 9th Indiana." He points to the dead. "This is my regiment."

Clay points toward the cotton field, "Mine's out there."

"And we're here." The Yankee points to the dead sergeant. "Do you believe in post-mortem consciousness?"

Clay's mind digs out Emerson, "The mind continues to function after death."

"I wonder if he knows you stole his shoes?" Bierce laughs out loud. "Wouldn't that be the dessert? He was a son of a bitch in life, so I say take his greatcoat."

After the two take the fresh overcoat off the stiffening sergeant, Clay leaves the Yank to his ponderings of this occurrence.

Careful not to get shot by either picket line, Clay moves to back to the Cowen House where he comes upon a silent commotion, ambulance corpsman loading a man onto a stretcher while others watch. As Clay comes up to the scene, he feels Tucker move up next to him.

"Who is it?" Clay can't see the wounded man's face.

"He took one in the arm. He was complainin about me dropping ass then he sits up. Just sits up. That's all. Sits up," Tucker deflates. "How'd the Yanks see him? Ain't my fault, I ain't feelin good. He just sat up..."

Alex! Just as the corpsman are about to take him away, before Clay can say anything, Alex goes limp. He watches as the corpsman double quick to the aid station. Hiram keeps a respectful distance.

January 3rd, 1863

The sun rises to men who have faced off for three days; frozen forms too tired to fight and too stubborn to run. On a small ridge Yankee cannon and infantry have formed behind fence rail and boulder while Clay's brigade shelters itself in a cedar forest of naturally made limestone trenches. Lying in formation, Clay is in the second rank of the prone, looking directly at Hiram's battered shoes. The macadamized roads leading to Murfreesboro have played hell on shoes, even Hiram's. The soul of his left shoe has separated from the upper, exposing a great gap of Hiram's foot to the cold and wet. Cutting the cape from his new overcoat, Clay wraps his friend's foot. The whisper of an officer alerts the company.

"Fall back silently. For God's sake, be quiet when you do."

"Fall back?"

"Yeah, damn it, and do it quietly."

Bodies slink to the rear, and the army begins its retrograde movement, the price of Braxton Bragg repeating Shiloh and Perryville—snatching defeat from the jaws of victory. Marching through Murfreesboro, Clay will never forget the intimacy of that woman, the spy, or Asa Lewis. Clay wonders if Alex is still alive. Clay will never forget 1862.

Bragg moves south to Shelbyville and the federals take Murfreesboro, so now Big Bob inspects blue uniforms as candles show through broken windows. It turns out Northern boys pay better than Southern boys.

Clay is alive.

Chapter Fourteen

January 5th, 1863

Clay's division commander rides up criticizing the sloth like pace of the retreat so the men quicken their steps. "No straggling in my command," he barks.

"Hey look, a horse with two asses," comes from deep in the ranks. The general rides on.

Starving men whose shoes have long given out struggle to keep pace. Starvation, cold, and generalship—most of all generalship—have beaten the army down to the nub. Those still in ranks slosh past hundreds of men lying on the side of the road cursing their situation and those who got them here.

"Old Bragg is hell bent on winnin," a voice yelps out.

Clay looks around at the sixteen survivors of his company. Hiram Stringer has a gash above his eye, the dried blood crusting the cut. Tucker walks without his brother. George Stewart limps from a spent ball hitting his shin. Clay chokes up for a moment and then chases away the emotion. Needham proves that men can sleep on the march. Barnabus Lazarus disappeared just before the battle, returned on the day after the battle, and now falls out, "Too tired to go on." Clay considers himself lucky, as his feet trod in fresh Yankee leather and bountiful wool socks.

George Stewart orders, "Close up. Keep your intervals." He lost his kepi so now he covers his ears with a strip of wool cut from his blanket.

The column comes upon a stalled artillery piece where the lead horse is sitting. Clay nears enough to watch the crew desperately trying to get her going again, the air blue with profanity. She's played out. An officer rides up, inspects the situation, then orders, "Shoot the horse and get this gun moving." The officer canters off.

Parallel with the scene, Clay watches a red-sleeved artilleryman pulls out his Spiller and Burr from an iron dyed holster. A pistol shot fills the air, followed by the tormented wailings of the horse being put out of its misery. The passing infantry salivates.

"Captain, mind if I get us some fresh meat?" Needham awakens, his knife already drawn. The captain nods his approval.

"Miller, give me a hand," Needham pulls Clay along with him.

Shoving through a growing mob of hungry men, Needham hands his musket to Clay, who watches in amazement as Needham makes quick work of a rear quarter of a horse not entirely dead. The gun crew looks on

in disgust as they watch their lead horse being carved up by
ravenous men whose intentions should not be trifled with.
Needham comes out with nearly twenty pounds of meat.

"Let's fry us some before the company gets it all."
Needham's crudeness is a role model on how to survive
in this underbelly of the world. Sentimentality nor
philosophical dissent need apply to a world where survival
is the highest order of life. Horse meat is better than no
meat.

"Hell, yes," Clay says and before long they have a small
fire going.

The army continues stripping the horse of everything
eatable while Needham runs his ramrod through a
chunk of horse flesh. Hanging the meat inches from the
smoldering fire, his face softens for he is, at this moment,
a rich man. A quiet solitude comes over him. The meat
cooks. The regiment marches further away. The fire warms.
Needham slowly turns the ramrod over the yellow flames.
Peace.

Clay pulls his bayonet to perform the same action.

"Boy, why in the hell you still carrying a bayonet?
They's useless."

"Good for cooking with," Clay offers knowing that's
not the reason. He carries a bayonet because...he's not
sure why.

"Nice shoes. Wher'd ya get them?"

"A bit of kindness from a Yankee officer."

"Well played," two men cook their supper.

The sound of horses destroys the peace. Clay looks up to see Bragg and his staff.

"You there," Bragg's voice attacks an unwashed, unshaven Texan sitting grotesquely astride a mule, smoking a corncob pipe. Squeaky and obnoxious, Bragg repeats himself, "You there!" Clay watches Bragg make another enemy.

"Who are you?" inquires Bragg.

"Nobody."

"Where did you come from?"

"Nowhere."

"Where are you going?"

"I don't know."

"Then where do you belong," Bragg insists.

"Don't belong anywhere," snaps the Texan.

Exasperated, Bragg asks, "Don't you belong to Bragg's Army?"

"Bragg's Army! Bragg's Army! Why, he's got no army! One half he shot and the other half been whupped to death at Murfreesboro!"

Needham grabs the remaining hindquarter, "Seen enough?"

Clay has.

Chapter Fifteen

March 1st, 1863

Today a warmth in the air not felt since early October embraces a blue sky. To improve morale, the captain gives the whole company a day pass with a reminder that Shelbyville, Tennessee is open for business. Clay unbuttons his jacket to scratch at a land the sun hasn't seen in months. Lice inhabits every crevice of the only shirt he has and they are particularly frisky today. *Must be the warmth has made them hungry*, Clay thinks.

Leaving camp, Clay and the Hogg Mess head past the camp guard and into the area between camp and town where, like the lice feeding off Clay, camp followers feed off the army. Whatever a man can buy is for sale here and the malnourished Army of Tennessee has a bit of fat in its pockets; a coveted silver dollar is plied for a new shirt. Needham trades a pair of fairly clean socks for a canteen half full of local brew. Everyone searches for deals amongst the vendors, laundresses, and prostitutes. Prostitutes. Clay remembers the green eyes of Murfreesboro.

"Hey mister, wanna ride my girl here?" a gnarled old man spews out amongst the flow of tobacco spittle. "She's as fresh as a spring rain."

Hiding behind him is a girl about to blossom into womanhood. She peers nervously at this collection of ragged soldiers. Pretty and innocent, she tries to hide behind her father until he yanks her to the front where, showcasing her youth, he spits on his hand then wipes her hair from her face. He offers her for a Confederate dollar a ride.

"You pig!" Clay smashes the old man to the ground. "Let's sell you for a dollar." Bile fills Clay's mouth. White hot fists pummel the old man's face. Clay loses control to a new emotion. Hatred.

"Get 'em, Clay," Stewart says, enjoying Clay finally having an emotional response.

A flurry of kicks, punches, and profanity assail the father of innocence. Fists pound out judgment. A child sold by a father. A volcanic heat builds. Lava flows through veins burning with anger, giving Clay a feeling of power he's never felt before. If only he felt this when the words, 'Hospital Rat' slammed into him. He feels the crack of bone under his fist. His mind returns to the night Mr. Miller pulled the knife on him. His mind fuels every punch with a memory of when he wished he was capable of this rage. Clay likes it. He wants more. He feels the gentlest of tugs on his arm.

"Papa. Oh Papa." The girl's eyes beg Clay to stop.

"Please don't hurt him anymore." She hugs her father. "Please mister, don't hurt him anymore."

"Shit!"

"That's enough," Hiram says, gently pulling Clay from the darkness of man.

Clay spits.

"Come on, Clay, let's get to town," Hiram leads him toward town.

As Clay and the others begin to walk away, a lady selling pies comes up.

"Wait, sir?"

Clay, still boiling, stops in preparation for some rebuke. *Is this the child's mother? The world is so fucked up, why not,* he thinks to himself. She looks at him with matronly eyes. He looks away. She takes his hand with the gentleness of a mother.

"Thank you for trying."

"Wasn't right," is all Clay can muster.

The woman pulls Clay's eyes up so she can see his soul, "That little girl thinks what's happenin to her is normal. What life's supposed to be? She think its love. Children don't know no better."

We do know better. Even the torn lives he's seen in combat doesn't compare with a child's innocence ripped away. And that's what burns in him. Hatred returns when the woman hands him something wrapped in a clean rag.

"What is it?" is all he can say.

"A pasty."

"What's that?" he is beginning to cool.

"A Welsh meat pie," she offers with pride. "Used to make them for the miners back in the old country."

Clay turns to see the child wiping the blood from her father's face. Kindness a few feet from pain, Clay feels a frustrated tear form. *Living in pain is different than causing pain.* Thanking the woman, Clay moves quickly toward the father of that girl, the child now standing defiantly between her father and the bastard Clay feels like.

"No mister," cries the innocent.

"Please, sir. No more," cries the father.

Stewart and Hiram attempt to catch Clay before he kills. Instead they see him hand the girl the pasty then walk away. Needham drains his canteen. The mess heads to town while Clay returns to camp alone.

Moving toward his cabin, Clay leans against a tree where he takes a long draw of warm air. Feeling the white heat that was so intense in him earlier cool, he feels his soul begin to calm. Another deep breath and he feels his body relax. A tightness, like a muscle flexing around his heart, slowly loosens. A half smile comes across his face. *What just happened?* He didn't get angry when Mr. Miller was choking his mother. Or when a knife was seconds away from ending his life. No fear, no anger, no revenge, no wondering why, he just took it like it was normal, or true, or deserved. Seeing innocence being sold snapped something inside him, and he's glad for it. It felt right.

"Hey, Clay."

It's John Jones, a towny from Highland who lives near the First Baptist.

"Good day, corporal." Clay offers politely hoping that's the end of the conversation. He sees a crumpled letter in John's hand, "I see you got a letter, best leave you alone so you can read it in peace."

Jones's face sinks. Clay stops.

"You okay?"

"I cain't read," he shows the letter. His eyes plead. "Never got a letter before. Bad omen, I fears."

Clay opens the letter, "It's from Pastor Stiles."

Dear Mr. Jones,

It is with heavy heart that I inform you of the death of your only son. The parish felt the icy hand of smallpox this winter and heaven has one more soul. Winfield passed quietly into the night with your wife by his side.

Sir, I have concerns for your wife. She has been inconsolable since Winfield's departure. The community has rallied to support her, and I myself have counseled her on numerous occasions, but to no avail. She will not accept God's will and I fear is about to enter the world of the insane. Since her collapse, your farm has fallen into disrepair and creditors threaten to put out your wife. She has no family in the area.

Sir, it would behoove you to come home and tend to your family matters. My congregation is large and in need of my council. This letter is my last act of Christian charity offered to your wife. She must now fend for herself like so many grieving

mothers have during this time of war.
God's Will,
Reverend Stiles

"What do I do?" Jones asks Clay.

This is the first time someone has asked for Clay's advice. He takes a deep sincere breath as he weighs what to say. Does he say what he thinks Jones wants to hear, or say what he thinks? If Jones runs away, he'll probably meet the same fate as the dead Kentuckian. If he stays in the army, his wife will die or become like what lay in Murfreesboro.

Clay offers his first piece of advice, empty really, but honest so he gives it, "You need to stand up for what's important to you."

Jones breathes in the thought then begins to leave Clay. He pauses for a moment then turns back, "You're a good man."

Returning to the cabin alone, Clay sits down outside the door, where he ponders the events of the last days. Once, while helping Dr. Hightower with a gangrene patient, he watched as the doctor poured acid on the wound. The doctor told Clay, "A caustic burns away the rot." New skin grows.

Chapter Sixteen

March 12th, 1863

Another warm day has Clay reluctant to button his jacket the way the army likes it—to the neck. He's been ordered to report to the captain so he buttons the top button only. Passing the row of NCO cabins, he moves to the officer's dwellings where he sees familiar faces. The army has been girding itself for the summer campaign by recollecting the men who have been away. Furloughed men with packages from home, hospitalized men with healing wounds, and coffee coolers with excuses for their absence are rejoining their commands. Alex has returned. He looks frail, but stands erect next to Stewart. Clay approaches, and their warm reunion is played out in a simple handshake with the other hand on the shoulder.

The captain breaks up the reunion, "Miller, you're first corporal now. Jones run off last night."

Clay hopes Jones has better luck than the Kentuckian.

"Corporal Clay. Nice ring to it," Alex pats Clay on the back.

Barnabus Lazerus pipes in, "Sure do. Surely do."

The company coffee cooler has returned. Since they joined up together, he has been the one to disappear at the first scent of gunpowder only to return well after the smoke clears. On the march to Shiloh, he twisted his ankle just as they were beginning the attack. He returned in autumn only to disappear again before Murfreesboro. Now, months later, he returns again. Normally, the army punishes deserters as soon as they're reported. Clay saw two die. Barnabus Lazerus has yet to be reported. Like a mongrel dog wandering the streets, his kind eyes and soft ways have endeared people to his plight, making him the pet of Highland. That plight was living the life of an orphan, doing odd jobs, scrounging food where he could, accepting the kindness of the church and community. The Currents would hire him whenever they could afford to do so. That protective benevolence has continued. Back home Clay too took a kind stance toward him. Not today.

"Where you been, Lazerus?" Clay questions in his best corporal's voice.

"Well, Clay, I took pretty sick, then after I felt better, they made me a hospital attendant. Kept me there till just a week ago. Said they were sad to lose me, but I wanted to get back to my people. Hope ya'll ain't mad at me."

Stewart rubs the boy on the head like a father proud of his son, "Good boy, Barnabus. You got back as quick as you could. No doubt about that." Stewart draws a look toward Clay, "Hell, Clay was gone, how long, before he come back from his Shiloh scratch?"

The perceived insult burns.

"You ain't no hospital rat, that's for sure."

Seeing Barnabus, his frail, cowardly, spindly self being admonished of a title Barnabus deserves strikes a chord of injustice in Clay. He feels jilted by the comparison of his time healing from a wound that almost killed him to a man who shows the white feather at the first sound of battle. Clay spits.

The captain turns to Clay, "Get some stripes, Miller."

Stewart gives Clay his first orders, "Corporal, have the men fall in for inspection."

As first corporal, Clay is the first one on the company line. It's a quiet position. He'll be more a banner to fall in on than a leader, but still it feels good because the men will dress right on him, wheel on him, and guide on him. It is a position of responsibility and he likes it.

"Inspection Arms," Stewart orders. "Prepare to open ranks. To the rear open order. March."

The rear ranks steps back three paces then open cartridge boxes so the inspecting officer can inspect ammunition. The first corporal, by virtue of his position as the first man in line, is the first inspected. Clay has never been good at keeping a clean musket. So long as the barrel's clean, he's satisfied. Clay properly hands his musket to the captain.

"Well, Miller, let's see if you have the sand to lead. Because of your height, you are first corporal. By your actions, you may stay in this position of honor." Taking the musket, the captain inspects the rusted barrel bands and hammer. Stewart offers a smile that faintly teases the edges of his mouth. The captain returns the musket then gives Clay a head to toe visual inspection. Stewart prepares to make notes.

"Musket rusty, but clean barrel, jacket uninhabitable, shoes acceptable, musket furniture serviceable," the captain states.

The captain and Stewart are about to move on when a sharp pain near Clay's genitals has him twitch.

"Stand still while at inspection," the captain barks.

The louse bites him even harder. Clay squirms.

"Damn it, man. Can you not stand still for one minute?" The captain likes a crisp inspection.

Another stabbing pain in Clay's crotch tests his discipline. "AARGHH!" he groans between clenched teeth as he drops his musket. Ripping open his pants, he thrusts his hands to the afflicted area then begins the scratch of all scratches. "Got one." He pulls him into the daylight then pinches him between his thumb and forefinger. "Bastard," Clay squeezes with all his might. "Die" With one mighty grunt he crushes his enemy.

"Miller!"

One hand down his pants, the other just having barely finished off a louse the size of a pinhead, the laughter of the company almost drowns out the captain's voice.

"When is the last time your body saw soap?"

Insolence borne from pain and frustration roar, "Before

Murfreesboro." Clay kills another. "When have any of us seen soap?" Clay grunts. The company laughs.

The captain looks to his company where he sees others scratching. Even Hiram shows the itch. Reaching into his haversack, the captain hands Clay a bar of soap then sends him and a few of the vilest men to the Duck River for as much cleaning as that bar of soap will support.

Excused from drill and fatigue duty, like children skipping school, the detail flies to the river's edge. Clay's coat begins the pile of greasy clothing he's lived in all winter. Next, his once white shirt rips as he attempts to unbutton it. Rotted. More rips as he unbuttons his cuffs. Frustrated and knowing this shirt is beyond saving, he tears the rotting remnants from his back. Throwing the rag in a fire left by previous bathers, its smolders its life away. It's at this point he feels the sharp heat of sun on his white body. Clay's been cold to the core since December; a cold no fire or extra layer of clothing could get rid of. Even the Yankee overcoat failed to warm him through. Only the sun can warm deep into a man, and today it's that kind of warm. Removing his shoes, socks, then pants, Clay stands naked in the sun. Like as a spring flower chasing the sun, Clay baths in the heat. His eyes close. His chin rises gently skyward. His breathing slows. An audible sigh escapes his lips. The world disappears.

A cold shower hits Clay. Shock. He looks to the river where Alex's and Hiram's mischievous smiles tell Clay what they've done. Wiping the freezing water from his arm, how funny his bronzed hand looks next to his white skin, he looks more like a puppet than a man.

"Clay, are you coming in?" Hiram follows his words with a mighty splash. "You need it."

"No thanks. I prefer the sun."

Barnabus Lazerus moves next to Clay, "I ain't goin in either. Dirt's better than cold, hey Clay?"

"Get in there and clean yourself. Captain's orders." Clay tosses the lye soap to a confused Barnabus, pushing him toward the river. Splash. Clay likes the power of corporal.

"Hypocrite," Barnabus whispers loud enough to be heard. "My boys are goin' to burrow up my brown spot," he blurts as the water hits his genitals.

Clay, still stinging from the 'hospital rat' comment, will not allow himself to be called a hypocrite. Splash. Dive. His body convulses from the water's icy grip and he gasps at the shock of it. In a hurry to get out before he freezes, he grabs the soap from Barnabus, making quick work of cleaning crevice and contour. A quick scrub of his hair followed by a plunging rinse and Clay is back on shore where he is clean and invigorated by the icy river. Warming in the sun, he leaves the frolicking of his messmates for a quiet spot on a grassy patch where he lies down. His limbs grow heavy. His breathing slows. His mind rests. He falls asleep. Deep asleep. For hours he sleeps in the warmth.

SLAP! Two handprints on his chest—white imprints on a red canvas. Laughter roars as Clay cringes.

Nearing sunset, the pile of greasy cloths calls to the

corporal of this detail. He orders every man to kill lice to their best design.

Alex takes as nap as Clay pries each lice individually from between the stitches then crushes them between his thumb and forefinger. Tucker tries drowning his by submerging uniform. From the woods, a sun reddened Hiram brings out a long stout stick consisting of one central length and two branches shooting out each side. It looks like a fan if it were upholstered.

"Lice don't breathe," Clay quips for all to hear.

"Lice are meat and I'm about to cook mine," Hiram laughs with a hint of country in his voice.

He takes his coat and carefully lays it open ended on the branch making sure the sleeves are inside out and not dangling. Everyone watches as he moves his contraption over flames, careful not to singe his jacket, he deftly pulls up a bit. He again lowers the coat within inches of the fire. 'Pop.' A louse explodes. Hiram's genius has everyone sprinting into the woods for similar sticks. For the next hour coats fight for space on the fire. Pops are followed by cheers then silence as all wait, wanting to hear the lice scream. Sleeves slip and burn.

With night upon them and having to get back to camp before tattoo, Clay orders his men to get dressed. It's here he realizes his mistake. Not thinking ahead, he burned his only shirt earlier in the day, so now he stands not sure what to do. His jacket's rough Osnaburg lining is far too coarse to wear without a shirt, and while most of men in his situation write home for help, he won't beg for help from a place that never has helped. Resigned to live without a shirt, he begins to put his jacket on.

"Here, Clay," Hiram hands his friend a shirt he bought the other day. "Should be your size."

Saved again, "Thank you, my friend," Clay says loud and proud.

Alex smiles. They head back to camp where they discover a box sent by Stewart's wife.

When Hiram's father sent a box of canned goods, the mess ate like kings. When Tucker received a letter from his mother telling of Alex's recovery, all shared in the joy. A common purpose and a common thread, each man has, at one time, shared something from home. All except Clay, but everyone knows why.

"Hope ya got some pickled eggs. I'd kill for a pickled egg." Alex then devours half a jar of what he hoped for.

Just then Stewart pulls a letter from the box. The last thing Clay wants to hear is Julie's words read by her husband. He begins to leave.

Alex brings him back whispering, "Julie's his now. Make peace with it."

In the quiet moments, Clay still thinks of her.

"Read it to us," Tucker chirps.

The cabin hushes as everyone except Clay leans into the upcoming words from home. Even Hiram joins in. The boys have always liked Julie's letters for she includes news for everyone in the mess. In this letter she tells of crops, church gossip, and the other frivolities of Highland life. Her words waft through their memories. In a somber line, she tells how Rut's children are getting along without a father's army pay. Rut's wife had to farm out each boy to a different relative—until she can find work. Clay wonders what kind of work this war widow will find. Julie even says hello to Hiram, of whom Stewart has told her about.

Clay's mind moves to their last time together. As quietly as possible, he rises to leave when he hears his name.

"Is Clay an officer yet," Stewart reads.

Clay's feet slow to the pace of someone wanting to be seen, his eyes darting to the calico curtains adorning the windows of the Allen family house, and their daughter Julie.

As a young man, he preferred the solitary world. He felt safer by himself, and except for times with Alex, he often sat by the river watching the ancient waters move to places unknown to the boy. It was there he first met Julie.

One warm fall day, as Clay leaned against a tree, tossing twigs into the river, a velvet voice called to him. "May I sit?" It was Julie. That first day, she offered to read to him. He said yes and after that, each day after school he and Julie would sit under that tree by the river, she reading her father's books and he imagining the waters traveling to the worlds her voice painted for him. Whenever she came upon an exotic setting, they would make up stories of what they'll do when they get there. When they would leave Highland.

That was until the summer of their sixteenth year when she went to stay with relatives in Tennessee. For the first month, just about every day, Clay went to the river to sit under that tree, imagining every detail of their time together, reliving every moment. After the first month, the words, the stories, and the images began to fade. Her velvet voice faded like bright paint on a sun soaked wall. It was then he stopped going to the tree, and although he thought of her often, he moved on.

That was the time Clay found forest work and the axe. At first, every swing said her name. That lasted another month. Molten metal when cooled hardens. Love when cooled hardens also, and so with each day away from her, Clay cooled until he found himself going into the woods with nothing more on his mind than learning how to be a good woodsman. He learned from Frank how to be at peace.

Then she came back and summer had changed her. Summer had made her a woman. And that changed everything. They met. She read. He didn't listen. His urges were too carnal for that. Instead of closing his eyes and escaping to the places she read about, his eyes imagined what lay beneath her dress. He watched her lips form words and his stomach tightened. She sensed it and turned her face away ever so slightly, her mouth only partially hidden. She felt the same. A gentle touch of the elbow, a hand wiping away a lock of hair, hands held on walks home. Each day their touching grew bolder.

Then one day, coming outside, she carried a worn copy of something. Her red dress form fitting around her small waist. Clay followed the front buttons from her waist, slowly past her breasts, to the black velvet cameo choker around her alabaster neck. They walked to the river in silence.

"What are you going to read me today?" the lilt of his words betrayed his desires, his eyes fighting to stay on her face.

"Lysistrata," she laughed a woman's laugh. "Perfect for the war talk going around here."

She sat first; then, after an awkward moment, he sat.

"'Good day, Lysistrata. But what has vexed you so? Tell me'"

The words pass by unnoticed, he concentrated on her breath. She leaned into his body, "I'm cold." He froze. The play continued as Spartan women threaten to withhold sex until their men stop going off to war. The sex, not lost on the listener, Clay began the physical movement that follows desire.

"No, Clay. This can't happen." The book closed.

Clay returned home to a letter in Mr. Miller's hand.

"What is this, sir?"

"What your mother always wanted. College. Ya'll leave in two days."

He sprinted to Julie to tell her.

"Clay." Her voice as sweet as ever. Clay bathed in it.

"Julie," he stumbled.

Her foot swayed back and forth like a child at a recital. He wanted to take her to the places they read about: Rome, Greece, Arabia. He wanted to take her anywhere so long as they were together. He searched for her eyes. She wouldn't give them. Instead they stood in awkward silence.

"You're going off to college."

"Yes."

Her lip quivered slightly. Her body became still in reflection. She stepped closer to him and looked into him with those eyes, those bottomless eyes. She looked deeper into him than anyone ever has or will. Then she turned away. Turning back for just a moment, she offered their denouement, "I'm Highland and that's all I'll ever be."

The boys laugh and pat Clay on the back.

"Not yet," Hiram offers.

Stewart reads her last words about Clay, "He's meant for better things."

Clay knows Julie will forever live in his heart.

Chapter Seventeen

June 16th, 1863

Clay moves on legs aching from malnutrition to the fire where he carefully mixes a handful of flour with water in his old tin cup. Kneading the dough so as to get every particle, he then rolls the dough to look like a snake. Next, he runs a palm sized chunk of bacon through with his ramrod. Taking his and Alex's bayonets for holders, he places the ramrod across the fire, just inches from the flame. Hungry beyond description, he watches the flame lick at his breakfast, dinner, and supper in one.

Next to him, Alex pulls his meal from his frying pan. In too few bites the entire ration is gone yet his hunger is not. Slamming his frying pan to the ground, he begins a tantrum that has his arms flailing about in violent protest to his condition and his feet kicking anything in his path.

"What the shit is that? Christ, I barely tasted it fore it were gone." He kicks his frying pan. "Why. Who needs a fryin pan when we can't even eat the shit we're guarding."

Clay knows Alex's point. For the last six hours the two

of them guarded a richly appointed field of corn. That's where Hiram and the rest of them are now, guarding corn earmarked for the Virginia Army. The entire area around Clay has been termed by Richmond as a granary for the Virginia Armies. Meanwhile, an army within eyesight of that corn is near starvation. Alex slams down his canteen and stomps off.

The silence of a storm just past sees Clay pulling his ramrod from the fire. Laying it on top of his haversack, Clay searches out Alex.

In 1861 the Confederacy claimed independence and Alex was the first from Highland to sign up. In 1862, Albert Sidney Johnston gave his life leading from the front. Then Bragg took the reins of the army. That fall he gave victory away at Perryville and again at Murfreesboro. Worse, he has failed to take care of his men. Starvation, ramrod discipline, and punitive rules have ripped the patriotic zeal from those eager volunteers like Alex. Alex, who followed every order as if it were offered from the pulpit, marched when told to march, fought when told to fight, and retreated when ordered to. He even starved when he had to. But this time is different. To starve next to a full field of corn reeks of hypocrisy. Clay has watched hunger and disappointment sap Alex's energy and permeate his every action. This morning Clay half expected Alex not to answer the morning roll. The night before he had talked about taking French-deserting. Almost everyone has and many have deserted. All except Clay and Hiram. Hiram, the one with the best life back home, doesn't talk about it at all. In spite of the chronic food shortages, Hiram has put on ten pounds of muscle. Simply put, the army has made him a more powerful man.

Finding Alex slumped against his tent pole, Clay comes up to him, "Hey, I have some extra pork if you want it."

"No, you don't, Clay. No one has." He disappears into his tent, the flap purposely closed behind him so Clay won't follow.

Clay returns to the fire where he finds his ramrod empty.

June 20th, 1863

The Yankee Army under Rosecrans has seventy thousand men coming this way. To counter those superior numbers, Bragg has ordered his men to create a line of earthworks from Shelbyville to Tullahoma along the passes and valleys of this hill country—over ten miles of trenches defended by thirty thousand scarecrows in grey. Today one third of the 7th Mississippi digs a ditch to protect them from Yankee musketry and cannon fire, while one third of the regiment moves about seventy-five yards past the ditch to work on impediments. The last third, Clay included, is sent two hundred yards from the ditch to make abatis. They will cut down trees, felling them in the direction of the expected Yankee attack. Then they will sharpen the large branches to a killing point. Finally, they will weave the branches together into a nearly impenetrable barrier designed to break up an attacking formation. Clay has never attacked an abatis, but he can see the benefit of them. He uses his corporal's stripes to take charge of the company axe. It's a battered version of what he used back home, but it's still an axe, and Clay looks forward to taking down a tree.

"Git after it, Clay," Alex chimes in. He has seen his friend with an axe. "Hiram, wait till you see this boy work his magic. Best woodsman in Highland."

"Frank was the best," Clay reminds him.

"He's dead. That makes you the best."

Grabbing the handle, Clay brings the blade up. A thought of Frank seeps in. *The best woodsman in Highland.* In a rusty arch, the blade meets the soft bark of a pine tree.

"What the hell, Clay," a disappointed Alex cries out like a circus patron unhappy with the show.

"I thought you were good at this sort of thing," Hiram chortles. "Maybe I should take a poke at it."

"Shut up," Clay blurts. Angry and embarrassed, he tries again. Barely a chip in the wood. Clay's power is gone. The near starvation of the last few months has left his body weak. The iron grip that used to roar now can barely hold the axe. He tries again and gets the same result. To end Clay's embarrassment, Hiram takes the axe.

"Let me try this thing." Taking a swing that reminds everyone of Hiram's city breeding, the handle splinters against the trunk of the tree, the blade almost severed. No more axe. "This is defective," Hiram demonstrates. Clay's pride is upheld by his friend.

Three men gather around the dead axe. Hiram smiles at what he's done. Alex pities the axe and Clay grieves the loss.

Just at that moment, the major of the regiment comes up to the men; Stewart and five fresh faces march behind him. Seeing the only axe in the company lying broken in the dirt sends the major into a rage.

"Who broke this?" Major Dwight looks into the eyes of the three.

Silence.

"Damn it, who broke this axe? How the hell can we get the abatis built without an axe?" he says pointing to the broken tool. Silence. Beginning to boil, the major turns to Stewart, "Fine, if someone doesn't come forward in the next five seconds, put this entire detail on punishment."

"Sir, that axe was about broke this morning. I'm surprised it lasted this long," Stewart tries to protect his messmates.

The major won't have it, for he must get the abatis built before the Yankees come. The major grabs the axe with its nearly decapitated blade dangling by a wooden thread then, using it like a knife, he points menacingly at Alex, Hiram, Tucker, and Clay, searching each man's eyes for guilt. Clay feels an old tension return. And he acts accordingly. He takes a step back, an action recognized as an admission by the major. He jabs at the air right in front of Clay.

"Sir, I broke it," Hiram steps up.

Turning to Hiram, the major jabs at the air just in front of him, "What's your name? I am putting you on report."

"Hiram Stringer."

"Jewish." A moment of silence. The officer launches into an anti-Semitic tirade. "You, Jew bastard!"

The major turns to those around him to muster up support for his venom. "This son of Abraham will be the reason this line fails. His kind killed Christ and now he's killed us. He's the reason why the Yankees will shove their bayonets up our asses!"

Watching Hiram being abused makes Clay white hot and afraid at the same time. Like the girl with her father, the injustice of the tirade makes Clay want to slam the major to the ground yet he doesn't. He begins to grow cold when the memory of how he abandoned Hiram before brings him back with a vile taste he never wants again. Taking a deep breath, Clay moves next to Hiram.

Alex steps up before Clay can speak, "You can stop now. That axe was a piece of shit way before Hiram touched it."

The major turns to the insubordinate Alex. "What the Sam hell do you mean challenging my authority?" He moves to Alex looking like he's about to strike him when he realizes the size of the private in front of him. He retreats to his tirade. "This Hebrew mongrel broke our only way to make an abatis. He," The major stops. He begins to pull his pistol from its holster. "He dies before we do."

Like a pride protecting one of its own, the entire Hogg Mess moves between Hiram and the major. A tension grows into a forever moment. At this naked moment where the artificial rules of rank and position are stripped away, this is a moment of man versus men. Looking into the eyes of the men who are now so close he can feel their breath, the major takes stock of his position. Clay moves even closer to the major and begins to feel lava flow in his veins.

Stewart works to avert the crisis. "Sir, we can get another axe from Captain Smith's company. He's got three or four."

Saved from the moment, the major steps away faster than his pride wants him to: a peacock plucked of its plumage. Throwing the ax to the ground, he moves to a safe distance, then turns to announce his authority.

Pointing to Alex, "Have that insubordinate son of a bitch carry a log over his head until his cowardly ways have him drop it. That should teach him some manners."

Alex has had enough. He grabs the broken ax handle and begins the movement toward the major. Fortunately, Clay and the rest stop him before he advances to the point of no return. The moment gone, Clay runs through his mind all that could have happened. Hiram could have been shot. Alex could have killed the major. Clay could have hidden in the dark again.

Tucker breaks the moment. "Sergeant, what you got with you?" pointing to four privates and one lieutenant sheepishly rustling behind the faded uniform of Stewart.

"New recruits," Stewart turns to the fresh faces. "Conscripts."

"Conscripts. What the hell we supposed to do with them?" Alex's previous anger carries over. "Bad enough to starve my ass off. Bad enough to have that piece of shit draw a pistol on me, now I gotta march with conscripts." He turns to them. Pointing a menacing finger into the face of the nearest one, "Where the hell were they last year, when we had a chance to win this thing?"

For a drawn moment both parties stare at each other. Yankee metal tore at Clay's face while these five were back home. Rut died on a frozen cotton field as they sat safe by their hearth.

Stewart introduces their new company commander, "This is Lieutenant Lee. Captain has transferred so Lieutenant Lee is our new commanding officer." For a painfully long moment no one salutes the officer until Hiram. Then Clay follows, then the rest offer the military sign of respect like men who believe the lieutenant should be saluting them. Alex won't. Instead he moves a six-foot log and hefts it over his head. Like Prometheus, Alex will bear his punishment like a man.

Stewart attends to the company, "Corporal, put these new men to work while I introduce the lieutenant to the rest of his company. " He offers a good natured barb to his pards. "The better part of his company."

Stewart leaves four fresh uniforms, complete with army kepis and intact shoes with men who look more vagabond than soldier. Alex, the log over his head, moves toward the conscripts. "Ike Clayton. In confederate grey?" Alex inspects. His arms begin to shake like he's going to drop the log on Ike's head.

Clay remembers Ike from Highland, from a unionist family. As the Highland boys talked about signing up for the Confederate Army, Ike had hammered all with his Lincolnite rhetoric. Clay admired how he was willing to stand up for his candidate. *He never had a pin though*, Clay thinks about it. Clay remembers, after one Sunday service, a couple loyal sons of the South escorted Ike into the woods. It took him a week to recover. From then on, Ike was a silent member of the congregation.

"Welcome to Phlegethon, the stream of fire," Hiram quips. Clay lets out the only laugh, and Ike stares dumbly.

"We'll cross the Styx in the morning," Clay says, he likes speaking the language of knowledge.

Instead of seeing Ike and the others as conscripts, Needham sees them as news. "What's the news from home?"

Seeing the conscripts in this new light, a flood of questions has the two groups intermingling.

Alex slams the log at the feet of the conscripts, "What's happening in Highland?"

"Have you seen my wife?"

"Did the crops get in?"

Ike ends the questions, "Yanks been through Highland."

Silence as they imagine Yankees in their homes, then Ike tells the group of the huge cavalry raid. "On his way to Baton Rouge, Yankee General Grierson headed to Highland to destroy the rail. There we was, in camp," Ike continues. "All the fellas like myself just joinin up." He emphasizes the word 'joinin' hard so all could hear it. "Learning how to be soldiers. Must have been four hundred of us in this camp out near Lick Creek; hundreds of tents, and all the provisions a fat man could want when up comes this rider yelling, 'The Yankees is comin! The Yankees is comin!' Just as we formed, here comes thousands of em, riding their horses down on us. Before we had chance, they had about two hundred of us captured—me included. The rest run off having barely fired a shot." He tugs at his collar, "I was paroled until exchanged. That's why I just got here." He turns to Clay, "After Grierson left, independent scouts, they called themselves, they did the meanness." Your daddy was teamsterin and, well, he came to town at the wrong time." Clay imagines Mr. Miller's scolding face. "They put a rope around his neck and dragged him through the streets till he looked like a rag doll." Ike closes, "We buried him best we could."

Clay smiles.

July 6th, 1863

The rain falls in torrents as the Tennessee River comes in view. Five days ago, the army was ordered to leave those magnificent fortifications and march south to Bridgeport. Retreat. Again, retreat. The first day of the march, the sweat poured and their heads swam in dizzied episodes under the pounding sun. Their musket barrels were hot to the touch. Clay's jacket felt like it was on fire. Mouths cried for water, but there was none to be had. At one point, Needham took his cup and scooped out the mud gravy from a wagon rut, thirstily straining the moisture from the dirt with his teeth. Clay followed suit. Other men fell out. Other men died. Everyone prayed for rain.

Day three, grey clouds on the western sky accepted their prayers. The first drop brought cheers and open mouths hungrily swallowing the sky. The shower cooled burning skin and invigorated tired steps. The men laughed and splashed in growing puddles atop hard pack. A lightning bolt across the sky brought cheers. A lightning bolt hitting a tree just off the road brought silence. A downpour brought mud and steps struggling to maintain their place in the line. It was here Alex called the army cursed. Everyone had a hard time not agreeing.

Today, the weather is humid and the grey skies threaten more rain. The crisp uniforms of the conscripts become as dirty as the Hoggs. Ike Turner marches next to Clay with a knapsack as full as the one Hiram carried into Shiloh. Like Hiram back then, Ike struggles under the weight of possessions better left home.

"Stay with us, Ike." Clay takes his musket. "It'll get a lot worse before you get used to it."

"Used to this? How does anyone get used to this?"

"I'll take this over freezing," Clay says, Murfreesboro

comes to his mind. "Better than the march to Shiloh." The sting of abandoning Hiram returns for a moment.

Changing the focus, Clay reminds himself that Ike is a Lincoln man.

"Hey Ike, you voted for Lincoln, didn't you?"

Clay can see Ike physically retreat from the question. He tries again, "What I mean is, did you ever get one of those gold pins that folks who supported Lincoln wore?" Clay feels his haversack for the poke bag containing his.

"Clay, I said my views and paid the price for it. No way was I going to wear a gold pin for all to see. Highland don't take kindly to people who think for themselves. Or disagree with their position. You know that."

From behind, Clay hears a splash and a cry. It's Lieutenant Lee. His civilian sinew not strong enough for this life, he lies in a puddle of mud, his eyes welling up.

"I quit," he whimpers.

"Me too," Ike echoes at the hope of finding a way out.

Clay watches Ike tend to the lieutenant like he's Florence Nightingale.

"What is the meaning of this?" The voice of the arriving major interrupts.

Seeing Major Dwight, Lieutenant Lee grabs his knee to accent his fighting ghost spasms of Herculean pain. Alex lets out a profane yelp at the disgraceful exhibition being enacted before him. Hiram watches like a scientists observes an experiment. Clay sides with Alex.

"Never quit," Clay spits.

"What's that, corporal?" The major snaps. Clay retreats a bit.

Looking up to the major like a dog begging to be let in the house, the lieutenant rubs the other knee, "Sir, I can't go on. Bad knee."

A private would feel the flat side of a sword for such behavior. Asa Lewis was shot for less. Clay watches to see what punishment will be meted out. Instead, the major sends Lieutenant Lee to the railhead to ride the rest of the way. Nothing. It appears the officers live by a fraternity rule of brother supporting brother. Really not much different than the Hoggs, who take care of and protect one another. Same here and as much as Clay wants to get mad at the injustice of it, he doesn't. Why bother? It won't change anything. Lee is not one of them. The major sends Ike to help the lieutenant. Clay doesn't accept this.

Ike and the lieutenant are off at a pace more energetic than their previous laments. Ike left his musket with Clay. Clay strikes.

"Hey, Ike," he booms, in a voice that stops movement. Turning to the column, Ike sees Clay holding the offending musket up high. "Might need this."

Ike sheepishly returns for it. Clay holds the musket just high enough to keep Ike from grabbing it.

"Please. Give me my musket."

"Why, you ain't ever going to use it," Alex jumps in.

The chapter of the quitter ends with Clay giving the musket back.

Ten miles later the order to halt has Clay and the others drop from exhaustion. Their bodies form perfect imprints of themselves in the muddy field. Morning roll call shows three more desertions in the regiment; two conscripts and a Shiloh man from Company A. Commissary issues a quarter pound of bad beef, four ounces of sorghum, and handful of cornmeal.

"No mail going home," Stewart tells the company. "Yanks have taken Vicksburg." While the Highland men lament their orphan fate, Clay sits silent for Highland was never his home. He has no home.

The regiment forms up for the last thirty miles to Bridgeport, Alabama. Two men die from the heat. Alex announces what most of them already know, "God must hate us."

Chapter Eighteen

August 7th, 1863

Bridgeport, Alabama. On its farm fields and woodlots, six hundred bone tired, hungry skeletons rest from their march. While the rest of the army concentrates east of them, Clay's brigade has been ordered to protect the army's flank by burning the bridge over the river and entrenching themselves along the southern shore of a river too deep to ford in this area.

Just off the shore sits a small tree-covered island whose strategic importance is its proximity to the pilings where the railroad bridge once stood. Keeping the Yankees from those pilings will, it's hoped, keep them from rebuilding the bridge. Clay and his company rest behind earthen defenses on that island. The Yankees arrived last night.

Across the river, barely thirty yards away, a Yankee soldier calls to the greyclads.

"Hey, Reb. We got no officer. Do you?"

Sergeant Stewart is in charge as Lieutenant Lee is still not with the company, "No."

"Well, then?" The Yankee private asks.

"A truce?"

"So long as no officers are about we don't shoot unless we warn the other."

Stewart accepts the offer for common soldiers to stop the war for a bit.

Minds relax as both sides have agreed not to fire on each other unless provoked. Released from their wall of dirt, the company rests. Some sit on top of their rifle pits watching the events across from them. Others cook what rations they have while still others write home, sleep, or whatever else a soldier wants to do during his free time.

"Hey, Yank," Alex yells across the river.

"Yea, Johnny, what you want?"

"Me and some of the boys wanna go fishin. Do you mind not shootin' at us?"

"We'll keep our guns cool." The Yankee spokesman lights a pipe.

While Alex, Tucker, and Needham attempt to improve their rations, Clay finds a shady spot under a willow tree, its long fingers waving gently in the river breeze. He lays down his blanket under the canopy of the tree. A few feet away, the Tennessee River flows in gentle ripples. The earth beneath his blanket is cool and dry. Across the river Feds splash each other, laughing like boys. The chorus of life softens. Life has gotten better.

"Hey, Reb!"

"What ya want, Yank?"

"Get your heads down, our artillery needs to clear its throat."

From across the river, a round flies over the island to land directly on a dilapidated building on the river road. Shards of clapboard rain pain down on confederate soldiers unlucky enough to be at the wrong place at the wrong time. Clay and the rest wait for the second round to determine their target. Bodies prepare to move quick if it's them. The next round makes it clear the Yanks are aiming for the town, so everyone on the island sits back to enjoy the show. Even the fishermen stop fishing to watch a round cut a horse in two, his front hooves attempting to gallop away from the pain. Alex and Needham laugh at the caricatured movement. Clay feels for the poor creature, a pawn of man, paying the price for being domesticated. Satisfied with their taunt, the fed guns go silent.

"Hey, Johnny Reb."

Alex rises from his fishing posture, "No more cannon play?" a cough prevents him from saying more.

"Na. No more cannon for a bit." The Yankee soldier moves to the water's edge to be better heard. "We got an officer who wants to jaw at ya."

Talking amongst the common soldier is more normal than not, but an officer wanting to talk is another. Stewart tells his men to hold fire.

Pulling a paper from a portfolio, the Yankee officer reads loud enough to be heard by the Rebels across the river:

From: General Rosecrans
To: All forces opposing the Union.

To any man who realizes the folly of his current path,
the Army of the Cumberland promises to any who
surrender to us, we will provide a fresh suit of clothes,
abundant rations, and, if possible, transportation home,
where said soldier will be allowed to live in peace,
without fear of imprisonment, or harassment, so long
as he promises never to bear arms against the United
States again.

Next to the officer a Yankee sergeant holds on high a
sack of flour. Clay thinks about making a ramrod biscuit
and how delicious that would be. Just to his left Needham
unbuttons his jacket, then removes the tattered remains of
his shoes. Socks then shirt. A splash and Needham swims
away from being a confederate soldier. No one tries to stop
him because, at this stage of the war, no man has the right
to challenge the patriotism of another.

Clay rises thinking about the food across the river.
Food. Not home. Just food.

Stewart walks up the willow, "Needham living with
Yankees," Stewart laughs. They watch Needham reach the
opposite shore. "Still, wouldn't be bad seeing Julie again."
He turns to Clay, "Are you going to join him?"

Clay walks into the sun, "Nothing in Highland for me."

August 10th, 1863

The best rations of 1863: half pound of near putrid beef, cornmeal, chicory, a spoonful of sugar, and a gill of lard per man. The mess devours its feast. Only one man complains today, the newest member of the mess and Alex and Tucker's cousin.

Neil smells his meat ration, the smell repelling him, "I hate beef. Salt pork don't go bad like this here does. What gives?"

"Pork is so much better," Hiram chides a man who doesn't know Hiram at all.

Neil perks up, "Damn straight, brother." Neil joined a group of men who have shared and suffered together for more than a year. He tries to connect with the one mess member he doesn't know. "I'm about done with this shit. This rawhide."

"My people do love their pork," Hiram says.

Alex spits out his cornmeal, Stewart snorts his chicory, Tucker laughs loud, and Clay, most of all, appreciates the joke. He likes the way Hiram fits with them.

Alex too likes this version of Hiram, "Boy, you sure have come out of your shell since Corinth."

"Oh, can't eat that either. Deuteronomy told me the other day, 'But whatever does not have fins and scales, you shall not eat; it is unclean for you.'" Hiram winks at Neil to tell him the joking will continue. And it does. The banter becomes a battle for position in the mess.

Neil asserts his position, "Me and mine need to get out there and shoot one of them shoats running around the woods yonder." He points to Alex and Tucker like kinship puts him on the same level as Hiram.

"What about your Hebrew upbringing?" Hiram stirs the pot.

"I aint' no Nebrew."

"We're all Hebrew, Neil, so buck up to the beef. Remember, you shall not eat of a beast of cloven foot unless he chews cud." Hiram's voice gets more confrontational.

Stewart steps in just to make sure everyone remembers the orders from Bragg, "No hurtin the locals. That means, no stealin their hogs, or chickens, or the girls' hearts," Stewart sounds official, yet he plays, too. "Besides, hogs are kin to the Hogg Mess."

Hiram continues the jabbing just so Neil knows his place, "Sergeant's correct, we shant devour relatives. My God, man, who do you think we are? Next you'll tell us to Oedipus our sisters." Clay watches Hiram enjoy this ribbing, "Oh, have you met our sister, Iama?"

Neil's looks confused and is growing frustrated.

"She's a Hogg," Stewart chimes in. "Iama Hogg."

Tucker knows Neil is about to burst, "I bet Neil wants to know if we had Iata?"

Clay watches as Neil looks more left out than he already is.

"A detestable thing makin fun of a man like that. I

need me some pork and I'll do what I need to get it. No more beef." He moves away in a sulk.

"No sense of humor in that one," Hiram's words are the last straw.

Neil moves to attack his tormentor. He would never touch kin, and Clay hasn't participated, so Neil flashes toward the one who started it. Neil coils like a snake ready to strike. Hiram stands frozen, not sure if Neil is seriously going to do something about a harmless ribbing. Clay's mind screams, *don't just stand there.* He wants to warn Hiram not to freeze before a knife. *Fight.* Mr. Miller's knife never cut, but it stabbed. Stabbed deep. Worse, the infection has made a coward of him. Clay knows what to do because he's abandoned Hiram before. *Never again,* he says to himself. *No more.* Tired of tasting that bile that comes from his weakness of character. *No more.* Awkwardly, weakly, unused to this course, Clay takes a step forward. His heart races. He can't catch his breath. His eyes stare at the blade. His fists clench unconvincingly. It's now or never for Clay. His mind wants to run, but his new decision pushes him forward. Neil's knife begins to move. *Better dead than taste shit again.*

"Eunice Livingston," Alex yells out to distract Neil.

"Bastard!" Neil screams. He drops his hand but still clutches the knife.

"Talk about a hog," Tucker joins. "Hiram, you don't know about Eunice, the pig-faced girl, do ya?" Turning to Neil, Tucker laughs, "Sorry, I mean Neil's love bird."

Hiram smirks defiantly, "Does she have cloven feet?"

"What so funny?" The knife loads again.

"Love bird might be inaccurate," Stewart joins in. "Nothing that big could ever fly."

Alex begins to say something when a coughing jag stops him.

Clay steps up, "I saw her get stuck in a door frame once." *Well done,* the voice inside tells Clay. For the first time in his life, he openly confronts an antagonist.

"Shut up, you shits."

Alex catches his breath enough to further distract Neil from Hiram. "Yup, she called old Neil there to butter her hips so she could get through the door. Seen it myself."

Neil returns the knife to its sheath.

Tucker finishes, "I've known Eunice Livingston for a while, and mister, if her past years reflect her potential, she's bound to double in size before you both hit thirty."

Neil storms away from the laughter. That night, just as he's about to fall asleep, someone sing out, "Eunice at the kitchen door. Victuals know she wants some more."

By morning, two more company men swim across the river.

Chapter Nineteen

August 12th, 1863

It hasn't rained since July, parching the land, drying up wells, and killing crops. Desertion, like a drought, parches the army; a third of Clay's company have already run off, including many of its Shiloh men. A hopelessness is pervading the army, partially because the new bodies sent to replace the deserters lack the character of the early-on men.

The one saving grace through this period has been the leadership of Stewart. With the gentleness of a mother and the firmness of a father, he has taken as good a care of the company as the conditions have allowed. He is respected and liked. Then, Lieutenant Lee returned, and each day he spews alcohol-fueled insults at Stewart and the company. His commands are often contradictory, or just plain stupid.

Today, before morning roll call, Lieutenant Lee calls Stewart and Clay to his side. Lee's red cheeks and unbalanced wobble shows he's an officer drunk before morning formation. His glassy eyes remind Clay of Mr. Miller.

"Sergeant Stewart," Lee is dismissive of the best man in the company, purposely looking away when addressing him.

"Sir."

"We have quite the mess, don't we?" he points to the men milling about. "Not worth a tinker's dam, the whole bunch. Am I right?" Lee looks directly at Clay. "Well, am I right?"

Clay stands silent.

Stewart redirects Lieutenant Lee, "What are the orders of the day, sir?"

"I see. That's the way it is. I see." Lee looks away. "Well, sergeant, the colonel needs a guard for the wagon train leaving this morning. Seems bushwhackers have emboldened themselves to do more than ambush single soldiers. Two days ago, they attacked a five-wagon train, killed the teamsters, and took the horses and the cargo."

"I know, sir. Those wagons carried the brigade's rations."

"Of course you do, sergeant. You know everything now, don't you,Sergeant Stewart? Pay heed. Don't forget your station, or your betters." He takes a drink from his canteen. "That's the order of things. Insoluble and forever." Lee angrily wipes his mouth of the burn liquor and life. "Understand?"

"Yes, sir." Stewart purposely searches out eye contact with the lieutenant.

"Yes, Sir. Of course, yes, sir," Lee mocks Stewart. "Of course," his thought trails off to a deeper recess of his mind. "Of course."

Stewart brings Lee back to the task at hand, "We can put first platoon in front with Corporal Miller, say ten rods in front of the lead wagon. Then I'll take the second platoon to cover the flanks." Stewart can see Lee's faint return from wherever he was. "Sir, we don't have enough for a rear guard. Can we borrow some men from Smith's company?"

Lee snaps back, his posture growing intense, "Get help. What are you trying to do to me? Ruin my reputation?" He straightens his uniform jacket. "Colonel said the same thing to me, like I couldn't handle my business. He said to me, 'if your company can't fulfill your mission, I'll send you some help,' he said. 'We will do our job,' I said."

"Yes, sir."

Lee moves to Clay. The reek of whiskey pickles Clay's nose, "How embarrassing that would be for us, if the colonel saw this in charge of our lead platoon." He puts a condescending hand on Clay's shoulder.

A growing voice inside Clay speaks clearly, "I'm not embarrassing."

Stewart steps in, "Shut up, Miller."

The rebuke burns Clay.

"Yes, do as your sergeant tells you. You listen. You don't talk. You say, 'yes sir.' That's all. 'Yes, sir.'" Lee pulls his hand off Clay's shoulder. "Sergeant, I don't want this man anywhere near this detail." Opening his tent flap, just before he disappears for the day he turns to Stewart one more time, "Put him and first platoon on picket duty. They can guard the road. Yes, I'll tell the colonel I'll provide a picket as well." He likes the sound of his delusion.

"Sir, we don't have enough to fill out the wagon detail."

The tent flap closes.

Later that day, Clay and his mess stand by the side of the road watching Stewart leading the remnants of the company. As Stewart passes, he gives Clay an approving nod. An action that catches Clay off guard considering the rebuke of earlier and the distant manner Stewart has been with him for much of the war.

With just six men, Clay must defend a picket line that requires a full company so he puts his assets where they will do the most good. He places Hiram and two conscripts on the road. Hiram is one of the best soldiers in the company, and a man Clay trusts. Alex, Tucker, and Neil each support a solo post extending away from the road south along a tree line. Clay will rely on their bloodline to connect the three posts set too far apart. To compensate for the lack of men, Clay will fill in the gaps by constantly moving between the posts for the next six hours. He begins by first sitting next to Hiram. He tells the two conscripts to watch the road so he can talk to his friend.

"Hey, Hiram, did you hear what happened last night?" Clay begins a running gag.

"No, what happened, Corporal?"

"Seems two women came walking down this very road. When the post challenged them, these girls came in nice as you please. Well, once in, one of the pickets tried getting friendly with the prettiest one." Clay stops to pull in the attention of the conscripts. "She was willing." Clay takes a dramatic draw from his canteen. "The soldier and the girl went off in the woods where her friend joined em." Clay gets up. "Well, gotta go check the other posts."

"So, what happened," questions the gray-haired, stoop-shouldered conscript. Clay doesn't bother with names anymore.

"Oh, they were Yankees dressed like women. They killed the guard. Gutted him." Clay rises. "Keep an eye out."

Leaving Hiram smiling and two conscripts attentively watching the road, Clay moves down the old fence row separating the field from the woodlot. A good picket line should have each post able to support the other, but with so few men, Clay is the mutual support. Only his movement between the posts will ensure any real security from Yankee or bushwhacker incursion into camp.

The wind blows softly today. The heat of the day cools in the shade of the woodlot. Bare earth indicates the trail between posts. Quiet, like a kid playing hide and seek, Clay moves lightly down the trail. He stops to listen. No sound. Taking a deep breath, the warmth of the day wisps by on a delicious summer breeze. Alone. What a rare and beautiful feeling. Alone. There is no peace in an army camp, with those thousands of foul mouths living foul lives in an army with foul intentions. Invisible to his mates and the world, Clay leans his musket against an oak tree, noticing the curve of the roots looks perfect for a weary back to rest. He looks around to make sure his duty is seen to, then he sits against the tree where the support on his back begins to relax him. He listens but knows that any bushwhackers in the area will be chasing the wagon train, not testing a picket line.

With solitude comes time to think. Thoughts and sights a mind should not want to remember return. Faces of dead men, grey in memory, come alive. Lice bites. Waking up next to a cold body. Frank's dead stare. Seeing those once powerful hands being buried under field stones. A search for peace of mind battles his experiences. Thoughts, the curse of the active mind. The whore's green eyes. His mother's vacant eyes. Grey rocks over Frank's body. Mr. Miller's knife.

Desperate to live in the peace that has shown itself in slivers and hints, he orders his mind to stop the shit. He breathes deep and slow until his mind quiets. Slowly, finally, he begins to notice the world in front of him. The glint of a web catches his eye as he watches the spider weave her gossamer thread. Clay remembers the story of Arachne. It was one of Julie's favorites. He hears her voice telling him, of Arachne's vanity, and her punishment for challenging Minerva to a weaving contest. In doing so, Arachne became a spider weaving beautiful tapestries with her silken thread only to have them destroyed by the whims of the world. Clay studies her work. Silken and perfect, he is in awe of the intricate weavings before him. Instead of tying Arachne's story to his life, Clay loses the darkness of his past in the almost transparent thread of the present.

I am the transparent eyeball. I am nothing, I see all, a quote from an essay rekindles a thought.

Reaching into the bottom of his haversack, he pulls out a grease-stained poke sack. Reaching in, he finds the Lincoln pin. Not the moment he wants to remember so he replaces it with the life stained remnant of *The Dial.* He begins to read, 'The smallest light illuminates the darkest day.' Clay remembers an experiment his professor performed. He ordered the entire class into a small windowless room. Squeezed tight, the darkness suffocated the entire class. Fear of the darkness began to grow until the professor lit a candle. That one spot of light illuminated the room and the minds of all who, just moments before, were afraid of the darkness. He then took the class into their well-lit classroom and dared anyone to turn on the darkness. Clay's mind recites the lesson, 'Light is the Good, and light destroys darkness. Evil cannot remove the Light.' Clay looks at the light peeking through the forest canopy. The rays of the sun remove the darkness from the forest floor, but nowhere does the darkness take away the light.

Clay finds the remnants of the essay, "Nature," where he discovers a line appropriate for this moment, 'The happiest man is he who learns from nature the lesson.'

Clay looks to man's destructive force, the path the pickets have worn into the forest floor. Nature wears the scars of the shell torn fields of Shiloh, the blooded cotton field of Murfreesboro, and even the picket posts of earth mounded over wood, scars nature will wear for over a hundred years and more. Still, nature will heal. The Shiloh fields will again grow green and cotton will again flourish in Tennessee. Timothy and clover have already begun to grow in and around the picket posts here in Alabama. Dr. Hightower said a caustic burns the infection away so new skin can grow. Clay realizes this journey is his caustic.

A chipmunk cracks an acorn. Journal put away for safekeeping, he heads off to his duties. Clay takes the wooded trail that curves around some sycamore trees and eventually to a farm field where he sees Neil in the firing position. Noiselessly, Clay slides up next to Neil. Searching the vertical forest for a man-made shape or color, the glint of steel, the sound of voices, anything that will tell him what Neil has a bead on. He finds nothing but scraggly corn, trees beyond that. Raising his musket to the aim position, he mirrors Neil's angle and height. He then draws a bead on an imaginary line from the end of the barrel to...

"A shoat!"

The pig retreats from Clay's exclamation when Neil's musket spits fire and the pig offers his final squeal.

"Orders are to leave private property alone," Clay snaps without fear of conflict.

Neil speaks up, "Na, Corporal, you got it wrong. This here pig advanced on my post, and when challenged, failed to give the countersign. With all the Yankee spies about, I just couldn't take a chance, so I shot 'em."

Bragg's orders, echoed by Lee tell Clay to arrest Neil. But in minutes, they have the pig dressed out and ready for transport.

Neil hefts the pig over his shoulder, "So, is this Iata Hogg or Iama Hogg?"

"Definitely Iama," Clay welcomes Neil into the mess.

"Soon to be Iata," comes out in a laugh.

Relieved from picket, Clay and Neil and the rest arrive in camp where the sight of a dead hog brings out the salivating hungers of the entire company. A conscript tries to cut a chunk off.

Neil swats him away, "Ain't right touchin kin thata way."

To bolster the meal, Hiram gives Clay the money to buy five sweet potatoes from a free black selling his produce. He appreciated Clay paying and not just taking them like so many others have.

Full bellies and quiet minds.

August 17th, 1863

Clay cautiously moves toward Alex's picket post. Bushwackers have been testing the picket line. He moves to within range where he should be challenged. He stops to listen. Nothing. The hunter in Alex would have heard Clay by now. Concerned, but not wanting to get shot, Clay advances a few more feet. Searching through the foliage, he sees Alex leaning against a tree his head dipped down like he's asleep. Clay moves up to Alex.

"Heard ya comin from way off." He looks up to Clay. "I knowd your walk since we was kids."

Alex coughs hard then immediately wipes his mouth. He coughs again, this time so hard he passes out for just a moment. In that moment between passing out and waking up, Clay can see a red bead on the corner of Alex's mouth. Consumption. He knew it, or suspected it, but now he knows for sure. Alex is slowly drowning in his own blood and there is nothing anyone can do for him. Clay sits down next to him.

Alex pulls his canteen to take a drink, "Damn it!" Tipping the canteen over, a few weak drops fall to earth. "Parched." Alex hands Clay his canteen. "Trade ya."

Doctor Hightower always kept the lungers in a separate tent so as not to infect others. And Clay knows sharing a canteen with a sick man is a guarantee of the same affliction. If he gives his canteen to Alex, what then? Clay, who is just starting to find himself in this world, struggles with the decision. He watches as Alex takes a determined breath, deeper than any breath he's taken in a while.

Alex looks to Clay. "Please."

Reluctantly, Clay hands over his canteen. Contents drained, a jagged cough spews pink mist on the spout. Alex hands the canteen back to Clay who tells him to keep it.

"Thanks, Clay." Alex looks at himself. "Ain't worth a plug now, I tell ya." He looks around his world, "Gonna miss it."

Alex's greying skin and the hollowed-out eyes remind Clay of the night Frank died. Yet, it doesn't. With Frank, Clay was the feeble boy desperately trying to stop the inevitable. This moment he is kind. This moment his thoughts are warm. His reaction human. Clay kisses Alex on the forehead.

"You sure don't need me takin care of ya no more, Clay."

"Thank you, Alex. For everything."

Clay has Tucker take Alex to hospital.

August 19th, 1863

A quarter moon night sees Clay, Hiram, Neil, and the two conscripts return to the quiet shores of the river for another round of picket duty. Hiram shares a post with the older conscript on the far end of the island while Clay takes the younger one and posts him near the willow tree. Neil is by himself, Clay's unspoken thank you for shooting that pig the other day.

This is first time on the island for Clay's conscript and the sight of Yankees milling about their side of the river has him uneasy. He puts his musket to his cheek.

"Don't shoot," Corporal Miller orders. "Those are Hazen's men. We saw them at Murfreesboro." His mind wanders to that frozen night searching for food and shoes. That Yankee officer who offered up the overcoat of a dead comrade. Frank too returns, but Clay stops the flood of dark thoughts before they again own him. He is becoming mentally disciplined.

The kid turns to his corporal. "Why don't they shoot?"

"It's my birthday. I asked them not to."

"It's your birthday?"

"No." Then softening the sarcasm, "The 1st Michigan Engineers plan on putting a bridge across here pretty quick. If we shoot at them, we just speed up the inevitable."

In the distance, a Federal band strikes up *Rose of Alabama*, an act of kindness toward their southern foe. Clay mumbles the words he knows, humming those he doesn't while the conscript struggles with what he expected from war and what he sees. He hears footsteps near the river.

"Halt!" the sound brings Clay back to see that the kid has his musket to his face. Clay pulls his hammer to half cock.

The conscript repeats, "Halt!" *This is a good one,* Clay thinks.

"Shut up, kid," comes a familiar voice in the darkness. Clay returns his hammer.

Stewart walks up, "Kid, go man a post with someone else. I need to talk to the corporal." Clay sends him to Neil.

"Not many of us left," Stewart says as he watches the conscript move off. "At this rate, won't be any left."

Both men stand in a pregnant pause when Stewart

begins pulling off his canteen. "You still don't have a canteen, do you?" He hands Clay his. "Keep it. I can get another."

A bit confused by the kindness, but glad to get a canteen, he accepts. Next, Stewart takes off his belt and cartridge box. Clay already has those, so he curiously watches as Stewart respectfully folds the worn leathers, as if he's getting ready for inspection, then places them on the ground. Next, he places his musket adjacent to his gear. Removing his jacket, he pauses for a moment caressing the sergeant's chevrons he's worn since the beginning.

"Clay, I like being a sergeant," he lays the jacket on the ground. Clay watches as George Stewart enters the river and then turns for a moment. "Take care of them." He swims across.

Clay hopes he and Julie have a long life together.

The next day Clay reports the desertion, and for it, Lee makes Clay Miller orderly sergeant.

Two days later, the long roll sounds, and the brigade heads southeast.

The 1st Michigan Engineers begins their bridge.

Chapter Twenty

September 8th, 1863

"If you're half the man Stewart was, you'll do fine." Dix says as he hands Clay six strips of black wool tape. "Being an NCO is something to be proud of, not to be hidden from Yankee view. Wear the stripes as a man would." Sergeant Major Dix emphasizes the word 'man.'

"Attention Company." Clay's voice speaks sergeant's words. The roll call begins.

By the end of the summer of the third year of the war, no regiment looks as it did in the beginning. Where once almost one hundred men filled out the ranks of Company E, now so few sun baked complexions stand for roll call; the replacements, mostly draftees, stand in fleshy contrast to the campaigned-hardened bodies of the veterans.

"Corporal Smith, Perry," a conscript from spring time, but a solid soldier and proof that not all drafted men are of low character.

"Corporal Cobb, Joseph." A Shiloh man.

"Middleton, Joseph." A substitute for a landowner's

son. His glasses are not strong enough for him to see the end of his musket.

And so, the new sergeant checks the names of those left in the company and an old face returned. Barnabus Lazerus. A shrinking army has forced Bragg to soften his ramrod stance on discipline. General Bragg has offered amnesty to any deserter who returns to the army. Asa missed it by almost a year.

"Lazerus, Barnabus."

"Here, sergeant."

Completing the roll, Clay offers a salute to Lieutenant Lee.

"Attention to Orders."

As the lieutenant pontificates about discipline, Clay looks across the parade ground where he sees Tucker half carrying Alex. They are going to try and get back to Highland so Alex can die at home. A tear begins to form, a tear for the loss of the human spark that was such a force in Clay's life. The world will be darker without Alex Current in it.

"Peace, Alex."

September 11th, 1863

Privates wear dirty uniforms of obedience. NCO's wear strips of cloth. Officers wear gold. Gold shits on cloth. Cloth shits on dirt. Gold bullioned sleeves of Austrian knots pass in and out of the headquarters Clay and his detail have been ordered to guard. This much gold traffic tells every private within eyeshot that the generals are planning the next bit of mayhem. Like a thunderstorm on the horizon, it's in the air. Inside a large tent, Clay's division commander holds a council of war with this brigade commanders. This is a perfect time for Clay to observe officers above the rank of colonel, and he's curious so he stands guard by the tent, his ears peeled to the sounds inside.

"General Anderson, General Deas, and General Manigault, based on the reports you submitted on the condition of your brigades, I surmise they are not in an optimal combat condition. Am I reading correctly?" General Hindman spouts to his brigade commanders.

"Sir."

"Yes, General Deas."

"Sir, the discipline of my brigade is suspect. They have not had a full ration in a fortnight, and desertions have cut my numbers significantly."

Clay's brigade commander, General Patton Anderson kicks in, "We've always been hungry and barefoot. Why cry over spilt milk. Let's see what we can do to act on General Bragg's orders. General Hindman, the High Pressure Brigade is ready for orders."

Bravery and bravado are the watchwords of Clay's brigade commander. *Ready for what?* Clay's mind calls out.

"Noble, General Anderson, if not a bit idealistic. If the men are unable to perform an order, how can we be expected to issue them?" Deas rebuts.

Anderson turns to General Hindman, "Sir, the men can follow orders, and will if we give them with purpose and alacrity."

Clay peeks between the tent flaps to see Hindman and General Anderson facing each other. Deas sips from a cup while General Manigault studies a map. From the day Hindman took over for General Withers, he's been hated. At every division formation he has spewed his secessionist zeal and self-proclaiming mastery of the art of war. Yet, every movement of the division since he took over has been cautious and contradictory and today Hindman's pedestrian military intellect is on full display. Clay's almost worn through shoes are testament to the miles marched since Hindman took over.

"By the spirit of General Bragg's orders, one can clearly tell he is no student of strategy. His juvenile treatise for our movement will surely lead this division to its demise. Generals, we must avoid any movement to McLemore Cove," Hindman lectures.

"General Hindman." Clay's brigade commander begins.

"Yes, General Anderson."

"Sir," Anderson interposes. "General Bragg is our commander, and that is clarification enough for us to follow his directives. Beyond that, he has a tactical knowledge we don't." Clay hates Bragg, but he can see Anderson's point. "We must work together if we are to beat Rosecrans back into Tennessee."

There is a momentary silence.

"General Anderson," Hindman clears his throat. "If I am to understand it, you have an adoration for the commanding general that many of us do not share." Anderson begins to defend himself when Hindman cuts him off, "It is my judgment that the esteem you hold for General Bragg has clouded your mind to the tactical facts of this campaign. I will not commit to a fight I'm not guaranteed to win." He pauses, "Unless I am given a direct order, then gentlemen, I wash my hands of the affair."

Clay returns to the guard fire, where he thinks about the future by looking to the past. Each general in that tent carries the blood of an army wasted. Each command decision made by men like Hindman. Each order has led to disaster. Shiloh could have been won if Bragg hadn't sent in his brigades piece-meal. Charging across that cotton field at Murfreesboro against a barricaded enemy got men killed and little else. Rut paid for that one. Those marvelous defenses at Tullahoma left untested. Bridgeport. Shooting men like Asa Lewis. Hanging spies, killing, dying, marching, failing. Clay can almost feel the vicious cycle coming back again. Will this next day have them charge a cotton field, or kill a man for going home? From out of the tent pours gold braid.

"Damned fool," General Deas spews as he grabs the reins of his horse. He lays whip to his roan, his staff struggling to catch up to him as he disappears into the forest.

Anderson and Manigault leave together. Working in confrontational whispers, they stop by the guard fire. Manigault hands Anderson a flask. "Well, Patton, being a Bragg man may not be the healthiest of ventures," Manigault states.

"Arthur," Anderson points back to the now dark tent, "Any wisdom from that ass best act as a road sign to the opposite direction."

He takes a swig from Manigault's flask, his face tightening from the effect of something powerful going down. Clay doesn't miss the pain of liquor. Gold braid rides away while Clay ponders tomorrow.

September 19th, 1863

Fall has announced herself with a northern breath: a sixty-degree day. All along Chickamauga Creek, confederates probe and parry with Rosecran's Yankee Army. All except Hindman's division, which is in reserve near the Lee and Gordon Mill. Reserve means being momentarily free from the bullets and cannonballs of the initial fight. Clay watches ammunition wagons head toward the sounds of battle while wagons filled with carnage travel the opposite direction. A local tannery offers its acrid smell to this North Georgia dust-up.

An ammunition wagon enters Clay's field and General Anderson gives the order for each regiment to fall in to receive ammunition. Not unnoticed by the general, Clay has his company formed before Lieutenant Lee can give the order.

"Sergeant, well done. You may go to the wagon to get sixty rounds per man." Seeing a bad officer next to Clay, he helps the sergeant. "Lieutenant, you have a good sergeant there. Let him tend to the ammunition. You rest."

"Yes, sir," Lee feels the sting of the rebuke.

Moving to the wagon, the green ammunition boxes alarm Clay. He offers his most appropriate epithet, the one he uses whenever the world is wrong. "Shit." Red boxes carry the sixty-nine caliber rounds needed by Clay's company.

Seeing Clay balking at the ammunition wagon, General Anderson investigates. "What is the problem, sergeant?"

"Green boxes. We don't have rifle muskets."

These words send General Anderson into a blue streak. Hindman sent rifled ammunition to a brigade of smoothbore muskets. Steaming from another example of his division commander's ineptitude, "Sergeant, are you a good man?"

"Sir?" Clay's never been asked that question.

"No time, sergeant, are you a good man?"

"Yes, sir."

"Good. Now get me some ammunition this brigade can shoot."

Jumping into a wagon full of the green boxes, Clay rides back to the supply depot. 'Good man' echoes in his mind the entire fifteen minutes it takes for the wagon to arrive at Catoosa Station: an unpainted depot of corrals, outbuildings, and scores of muddied tents filled with the supplies of war. Empty wagons move to the appropriate piles of supplies while filled wagons leave for their brigades.

After making sure the right ammunition is sent to the brigade, Clay goes off to explore. Always hungry, he's surrounded by barrels of salt pork stacked sky high along side mountains of grain sacks. Moving to the commissary area, he passes men butchering emaciated cows, blood up to their elbows, vile men throw hunks of meat into barrels black with flies that darken the skies every time a hunk of beef lands. That meat will eventually find its way to Clay's haversack and for that, he wishes he hadn't seen what he just saw. Moving past sacks of cornmeal and mountains of potatoes, Clay sees a familiar face inside a tent. Hunger moves in.

"Haven't seen you since October last." Clay fights to remember his actual name. The disinterested look of Tennessee does not bode well. Clay doesn't quit, "I was wondering what happened to you." Looking around the tent like it's a castle, Clay feigns impressed. "See you got a good job goin' for yourself. Good to see."

Tennessee gives a quick look at Clay, and then decides he doesn't remember the scarecrow in front of him. Haggard Rebs constantly work him for a handful of cornmeal or a sweet potato. Clay is just one more leech to him.

"Have you seen Doctor Hightower?" the question opens the door.

"Miller?" Tennessee says, recognizing the emaciated sergeant before him. He softens in reminiscence of a quieter time. "Sure do miss the quiet of that that camp: you, me, Milford. Even your man was a good sort." He pauses. "What was the name of your darkey?"

"Frank." Clay's chest tightens.

"Where is he?"

"Dead." The cold of that night returns.

"Sorry to hear it. He was a good one."

Clay begins to tell the story of that October morning, almost glad to share a story with someone who had a kindness for Frank when Tennessee pushes three sweet potatoes into Clay's hands, and before Clay can recognize the condolence, or finish his story, Tennessee is back to his forms. Clay moves away.

The sound of a train whistle pulls Clay toward the tracks where he sees steam spewing from a rusting locomotive as it brings in more than it was designed to pull. The train stops, and in moments the first part of its cargo disembarks: a color bearer jumps off the train, his red banner swinging to the cheers of the soldiers joining him on the ground. The grapevine around camp has talked about the whole Virginia Army coming to Georgia. Even Joe Johnston's army is rumored to be arriving soon to help Bragg with his Yankees. As the Saint Andrew's cross waves its figure eight, Clay reads the battle honors painted white on the red cloth, *Gettysburg*.

"Sergeant."

Clay stares at the flag. *Gaine's Mill.*

"Sergeant."

Sharpsburg.

A meaty hand touches his shoulder.

"Sergeant!"

Looking up to a mountain of a man, Clay sees gold bullion underneath a massive black beard.

"Yes, sir," Clay salutes.

"Which way to General Bragg's headquarters?"

The power resonating from this general has Clay standing at attention. The meaty hand stays on Clay's shoulder, "Son, can you direct me to General Bragg?"

Clay turns and points up the road, "About nine miles up that road."

The general's face tightens in an unmistakable reaction to Braxton Bragg.

The general turns to a young captain, "Please inform the brigade commanders, when they arrive, that I'll be headquartered," he looks around for a suitable spot in the sea of confusion.

Putting his sweet potatoes his haversack, Clay begins to walk away when an innate need to help has Clay returning. "Sir, there's a creek about a quarter mile up that road there." Clay points to the road he recently travelled. "Not too far down, there's a large field off to the left and an oak tree with plenty of shade for your headquarters."

The general smiles, "A shade tree will suit me fine." He turns to an aide, "Direct our generals, we have a rendezvous point. Tell them we are heading down that road."

"Yes, General Longstreet," and off the aide goes to find other Virginia gold braid.

Longstreet. General Longstreet, the best corps commander in the South's most successful army. Everyone in the South knows James Longstreet, not by face, but certainly by reputation. 'A hero to Southern hopes' the newspaper calls him. He crushed a Yankee Army at Second Manassas. He stopped another at Sharpsburg. He even fought game at Gettysburg. Clay watches this hero of the Confederacy certainly looking and acting the part. Unlike General Hindman, Longstreet resonates command. And now he's here. Hope lights a candle in Clay.

He's curious about a man who is larger than life both figuratively and physically. A thousand questions come up, yet Clay asks none. He knows his place. Clay again begins to leave when the booming voice calls him,

"Sergeant. Do you think your colonel would mind if you joined my staff for a bit?" he smiles. "Sure could use your help."

Clay Miller proudly leads General Longstreet down a Georgia road to a field with a stream and a tree where the general inspects the area Clay's chosen. Longstreet nods in approval then lays down under the oak tree. Closing his eyes, he takes a nap, leaving Clay alone in an almost palpable awkwardness. *Do I return to my regiment, or stay here?* Duty has him heading back to make sure the right ammunition gets to the brigade, yet a curiosity has him wanting to stay. Clay has seen one council of war and now he wants to see another. This time from a general who wins. Everyone in Bragg's army knows what the Army of Northern Virginia has been doing. For Clay's Shiloh, Longstreet had the Seven Days Campaign. For Clay's Murfreesboro, the Virginia Army had their Fredericksburg, and so on. No one in Clay's army will ever say the Virginia Army is better, but something makes them just that, and Clay wants to know what it is.

The general's voice brings Clay out of his inner dialogue. "Sergeant, if I remember correctly, you had some sweet potatoes in your hand when we first met."

Hunger wants to protect food, Clay wants to share.

"Any chance of our sharing your meal?" the general smiles knowing rank has its privileges. "I haven't had a sweet potato since I don't recall when."

"I'll get a fire going." Purposely putting the fire close to the tree, Clay listens as a steady stream of officers arrive and thousands of victors of Manassas, Fredericksburg and Chancellorsville fill the field. A new general's braid arrives.

"General Longstreet."

"General Kershaw, trust you had an uneventful journey."

They shake hands like men who respect each other. Clay listens as they discuss the military situation. Longstreet is clearly in charge as every subordinate listens intently to orders, then departs to do as ordered. Clay compares this to the meeting at Hindman's tent; the jagged dialogue and the tension in the air whenever Bragg's name was mentioned, the backstabbing of division commander to army commander, brigade commander to division leader. In Longstreet's command, everyone Clay has seen is accorded a professional respect.

"General Humphrey's, good to see you. What is the fighting condition of your men?"

"Ready to lay into them, general. Just tell me where to go."

"I'll have to wait on that. It appears General Bragg is too busy with his affairs to send us a guide," Longstreet stretches his back. "We must see to our troops and prepare as best we can. From the sounds of it, we will be in a fight soon enough," Longstreet cautions.

"God willing, general."

"In the meantime, get your men fed."

Clay pokes at the potatoes with his bayonet. Still not entirely done, he moves to the creek to fill his canteen. Passing a regiment of Longstreet's troops cooking rations. Clay compares these men to the ones he serves with. They cook and move about just like the 7th, frying up salt pork and boiling rice. Yet the cynicism of Clay's camp is absent here. They have a confidence, almost a cockiness that is off-putting to Clay on one level, yet appealing on another. While they wear new uniforms of a grey blue wool, Clay's threadbare jean cloth resonates hard times. They chuckle and point at him, for they no doubt have read the stories of Shiloh and Murfreesboro. The result of a battle is the shingle worn by the army. The Virginia Army wears the shingle of victory, while Clay's army wears the shingle of defeat after defeat. If he had joined the University Greys, he and Hiram would have fought in the Virginia Army. Instead, he joined with his Highland friends. To be a sergeant in an army with a bad reputation is a shingle that has Clay embarrassed to wear his stripes. He feels like a hospital rat again.

Arriving at the creek, he moves amongst Virginia men filling their canteens and washing themselves. Keeping himself as low key as possible, he kneels down and begins to fill his canteen. Next to him, a lieutenant corks his.

"How you faring, sergeant?"

"Fine, sir."

The lieutenant winces at the word *sir*, "Not used to that yet. Spent most my time like you, a sergeant." They shake hands.

"Good to have you Virginia boys with us," Clay offers politely.

"None of us is Virginia people. We left them back with Marse Robert. Longstreet has all but Virginia. I'm Kirkland. 2nd South Carolina."

"Miller, 7th Mississippi."

Clay's canteen fills quickly, "I better get back. I'm cooking sweet potatoes for your General Longstreet."

"Sweet potatoes, you say," Kirkland responds. "Potatoes of any kind are a luxury in Virginia. Sure, do miss em. We tend to get a lot of rice."

"I have three just about cooked through. Your general

only needs two. If you want one, I'll trade it for your rice."

Kirkland stands straight, as if at attention, "Na, you give em all to General Longstreet. He'll need the energy." Kirkland nods then moves off.

"I'll be damned." *Selflessness is beautiful.*

Potatoes done, Clay stabs all three potatoes with his bayonet then moves to the tree.

"Sir, they're done."

Longstreet's eyes light up as he moves toward the steaming meal. Clay tips his bayonet. The first two slide off, their skin not too crisp, the insides soft and ready to eat. Self-preservation has Clay pull up before the third falls then, but hearing the voice of Lieutenant Kirkland in his head, he lets the final one drop.

"Thank you, sergeant." Longstreet devours them like the big man he is. Wiping his mouth, he lets out a long delicious sigh. Looking up to Clay, he inspects the tattered uniform and the ragged shoes. "I see you are in need of a pair of shoes, and maybe a new jacket." He looks at Clay's cartridge box. Made of cloth, it hangs limp, a sad ode to ersatz. "That cartridge box must be tough to pull a round from."

"Yes, sir."

"Colonel Manning, is our quartermaster up?"

"Yes, sir. Came on General Kershaw's train. Your horse is up as well. And your personal commissary."

"Kindly take this man to the quartermaster and get him whatever uniform items he needs." Longstreet smiles,

"As a thank you for these fine potatoes, and for finding this excellent concentration point for my corps."

Clay gives the best salute of his military career.

"And get him a pound of that Nassau bacon from my chest." He puts his hand on Clay's shoulder; then, in a father's voice, he says, "Too bad I have to return you to your army. We could use a good man like you." Duty calls Longstreet away, leaving Clay bathing in the sentiment.

The shirt Hiram gave Clay back in March is replaced by one made in England. His well patched pants find themselves in a pile along with his greasy jacket, each replaced by English-made blue/grey wool snuck through blockade then given to Longstreet's corps by the governor of North Carolina. Putting on the new clothes, Clay likes the cut of the jacket and beams at the military look of the epaulets and the complete set of brass buttons. Unfortunately, it appears even the Virginia Army is short on shoes. Clay continues his journey on the leather kindness of that Yankee officer at Murfreesboro.

Moving down the road to the Lee and Gordon Mill, Clay basks in the newness of his uniform and equipment. Even his smoothbore has been replaced with an Enfield rifled musket.

From behind him he hears horses. General Longstreet and his entourage ride past. Clay purposely puts himself in their way. Longstreet sees him.

"You look like one of us now."

Clay is about to tell the general if he had joined a month

earlier, he would be marching with Longstreet, but stops before he embarrasses himself. "Do you have enlistment papers for me to sign, general?"

"Not at this time, sergeant," he enjoys Clay's confidence. The stern face of frustration replaces his momentary levity. "Its five o'clock and I still haven't found your commanding general. Any idea where his headquarters are?"

The last Clay knew, Bragg was by the tannery so he points in that direction.

"Good man." Pulling his horse around, he looks at Clay, "Shoeleather and the bayonet will win the day, sergeant." Longstreet heads off to find Bragg.

Sunset means a cool day will turn into a chilled night. Clay finds his regiment just as the darkness takes away the colors of the day, yet enough light remains for his mates to tease him about his new clothes.

"Looks like you done joined them Virginia fellers," Neil spews.

"Just remember, well-tailored clothes don't make a soldier," Hiram chides Clay.

"Sides them Easterner ain't fought the Yanks we got," Neil brags.

"I think they'll do alright." Clay wants to tell them of the confidence he saw in their camp, and the professionalism of their officers. He read their flags. The 7th flag illustrates Shiloh, Perryville, Tullahoma—good fights with bad results. His army doesn't have a Longstreet.

No fires allowed, the night chill has the Hogg Mess

spoon. Hiram's and Neil's threadbare bedding are placed under the three then Clay's new tan wool blanket covers them all. Toasty. As the other two fall asleep, Clay thinks about the day. *Good man.* Two generals said, 'good man' to him. He's not sure what he did or how recent events came about, but it doesn't really matter, for today was a good day and Clay's happy with that. He hears the chattering teeth of Barnabus Lazerus so Clay invites him into the Mess.

Chapter Twenty-One

September 20th, 1863

Frost shimmers in the North Georgia dawn. Pulling himself from his cover, Clay is one of an army beginning to stir. An aide rides past, searching out generals. A battery moves into position to begin their Sunday desecration. Clay pulls his new musket from his blanket. *God must cry at what his children do to each other on the day dedicated to Him*, he thinks as he looks down the barrel at the well-honed grooves of the Enfield musket given to him by Longstreet's ordinance people. Clay never had to shoot at Shiloh. At Murfreesboro he emptied his cartridge box of its forty rounds each day he fought without ever aiming at one person. He took solace in that. He knows he doesn't have that killer in him. Only once did he feel anger deep enough that maybe he could have killed a man, but that ended with the gentle touch of a little girl protecting her father.

Putting the musket down, he takes the stripes he pulled off his old jacket and begins sewing them on his new one.

Faded and rather ratty, it's almost a disgrace to put them on this fine English cloth. Not even a stain on it. Still, the stripes are the rank, so he puts them on. Needle to thread, he finishes and then looks smartly at his handiwork. They are straight and evenly spaced. *Well, there's that,* he thinks to himself. This will be his first battle as a first sergeant. He looks back to his Enfield and smiles just a bit. First sergeants don't fire their muskets. They keep the men on the firing line. They make sure they do as the officer orders. He feels Barnabus snoring next to him. They make sure *every* man does his duty. *Yes, he will do his duty today.*

"Sergeant Miller."

"Yes, Lieutenant Lee." Covering up Barnabus, Clay offers the obligatory salute. "Sir."

Lieutenant Lee looks at the mounds of blankets that make up his company, "I have an officer's meeting." He responds then heads off. "Oh, take the roll."

"No shit," Clay mutters.

"What's that?" Lee turns to what he sees as an affront to his position.

"Shoeleather and the bayonet will win the day, sir," Clay salutes.

"You are an odd sort, sergeant. I have no idea what you are talking about."

"Yes, sir."

Clay takes roll call by the blanket. Each blanket is a man. He lets them sleep a little longer. They'll need it. Yesterday was the opening round of what will become a big fight and Clay is looking forward to it. Unlike his past battles, he feels like he can make a real difference in this one. Sergeants won't win battles for sure, but they can keep a small group of men moving in the right direction. Besides, with Longstreet here, he feels an optimism. He likes the taste. The Virginia Army doesn't lack for optimism. Proud, almost arrogant, they march with a swagger Clay finds himself attracted to. Clay thinks about that South Carolina officer he met by the creek. He found himself instantly impressed with Kirkland—a good man of purpose. Today Clay wants to fight as well as the Virginia Army. He wants to see his flag lettered white with a victory. Clay heads to regimental headquarters for sergeant's call where he announces, "all present."

After the meeting Clay returns to a company up and getting ready for the day. Some men warm themselves by small fires while others prepare for an uncertain future. Clay finds Hiram next to the fire cutting up a sweet potato. Reaching into his haversack, Clay pulls out the pound of Nassau bacon General Longstreet gave him. As much as the boys made fun of his new uniform last night, they sure enjoyed his warm blanket, and they will feast on the bacon. Clay tosses it to Hiram.

"Bacon. Where did you get that?"

"General Longstreet gave it to me."

Neil comes up from the covers, "Bullshit. You stole it from some commissary."

"I didn't have to steal," Clay says, but winks to Hiram,

"Tell you what, Neil, if Hiram cuts up that potato, and if you go fetch water, I'll share my bacon with you." He points behind him, "There's a creek just through those woods."

The thought of bacon and sweet potatoes has Neil up and halfway to the creek before Hiram calls him back for his canteen. Ever since the knife incident, Hiram doesn't suffer Neil very well. Since Alex and Tucker left, Neil has lost some of his starch. The Hogg Mess is the only home he has. Hiram throws his canteen at Neil's head, but before Neil can draw blade again, Clay steps in.

"Hurry, Neil, or we'll eat without you."

Canteens rattling, Neil is off at a canter. Clay sits down next to Hiram and begins slicing the bacon, using his thigh as a cutting board.

"Clay, you do tempt fate. What would happen if you cut yourself? Infection. Amputation. Don't leave me here with that lout."

"Know what?" Clay offers.

"What?"

"That creek's about a half mile away."

Hiram smiles, "Too bad for Neil." The sound of skirmishers at play drifts in from the far right as Clay hands over the sliced meat then gets up.

"Gotta go check on the company."

"I'll have a plate for you when you get back."

Moving just a bit away from the company, he calls the one other NCO to him. Placing his hand on Corporal Perry's shoulder, he gives his orders. "It's going to be up to you and me to keep the company in line—to keep an eye on the rear rank." Even Clay is impressed with how official he sounds, a bit like Stewart. "Make sure we keep thirteen inches between ranks so the front rank doesn't get shot by their file-mates."

Perry dismissed, Clay moves about the company.

Private Cobb uses the Augusta Argus to protect his eyes from the rising sun.

"What's in the news?" Clay asks.

"We're going to win the war this week." Cobb turns the page and reads, "No wait, now we're going to lose the war this week."

Off to the left, Private Middleton caresses an ambrotype of his wife. Private Rushing turns the page to a letter he's read a hundred times. Private Wells and Private Sermon hover over a New Testament. Wells is the faster reader so he patiently waits for Sermon before turning the page.

"What verse?" Clay feigns pious.

Wells recites one from memory, "He himself calls out to me…" Sermon joins in, "You are my Father, my God, and the Rock of my salvation. Psalms 89:26."

They begin to homily as Clay moves to Private Algood who wipes the rust from his musket. Private Mann squeezes a louse out of existence. Private Adams sleeps. Clay checks each man in the company to make sure they're ready. Satisfied with what he sees, he returns to his pards.

"Just about done," Hiram says as he tends the bacon from the pan. "If we hurry, that brown spot Neil won't get any." Then he points to Barnabus slithering towards the woods. "There that one goes again."

"What does Dante say about guys like him?"

"Dante doesn't, Clay. Dante deals with sinners who do or do not repent." Turning the bacon, "Oh, except for, maybe, the Opportunists, but he isn't that."

"Why not. He's the perfect Opportunist. He is a good soldier in camp, keeps up on the marches, does his duty whenever called on, but come the hint of gunpowder, off he goes into the unknown."

Pulling the frying pan from the fire, Hiram looks at Clay, "Surviving isn't a sin. It may even be the actions of a saint."

Clay begins to move toward Barnabus, "He ain't no saint."

"Who is?"

Clay sprints up to Barnabus, "Where ya going?" Frozen, Barnabus stares at Clay with eyes begging to let him go. *Not today.* An artillery round lands about eighty yards to the right of the two. Barnabus ducks. Clay smiles at his lack of soldierly knowledge. Clay educates, "They do that once in a while. They'll send a shell over to see if we'll stir. That one is too far away for us to stir."

Barnabus starts for the woods.

"Where ya goin?"

"Gotta make water."

Placing himself in front of the woods, Clay points to the sink not ten feet from Perry, "Go there if you have to."

Then he points toward the sound of cannon, "We'll be pitching in soon. And we'll need your musket today."

Defeated, Barnabus returns to Clay's blanket, where he covers himself up like a child hiding from a storm. Clay returns to the fire, where he sees Neil dropping the canteens.

"Know what the Indians call that creek back thar?" Neil takes a breath. "River of Death. Heard that from a fella heading out."

Hiram deepens the allusion, "Dante has the River of Blood."

The communal meal of bacon, fried sweet potatoes, and a half-cup of peel coffee per man fills the stomachs of the Hogg Mess. Neil burns his lips on the coffee. Hiram carefully layers a piece of bacon and a slice of potato on his fork then enjoys it like an epicurean feast. Barnabus stares at his plate like a condemned man at his last meal. Clay savors every flavor in slow, purposeful chews. Off to the right, the sound of battle intensifies.

"Last supper," Neil streams spit through the gap between his two front teeth.

Barnabus lets out a deep, sad sigh.

Suddenly, the sound of a dozen drums beating out their powerful call to formation sends chills through the fearful and white heat through the warriors. From their repose, thousands upon thousands of Southern boys rise up to the call of war. Chaos becomes order as linear formations grow. Flag bearers offer their charges to the sky as companies form to the regiments, regiments form to the brigades, and brigades form to Hindman's division. Two hundred yards to Clay's front, almost a thousand South Carolinians in Manigault's brigade resonate the metallic reaction to the order, "Fix Bayonets."

"Center Dress," Clay's colonel shouts, his voice cracking from the intensity. "Order Arms."

Clay watches as his company follows orders. *We're crisp today.* The drums stop and a hush falls over the field. In mere moments, The Army of Tennessee, two division of the Virginia Army, and other troops drawn from across the Confederacy will attack an enemy Clay has seen twice. The weight of the musket pulls at Clay's right hand. The weight of the stripes increases. Standing in the rear rank, immediately behind Lieutenant Lee, Clay sees shaking hands reach into a leather haversack as Lee pulls a pewter flask out and gulps courage before putting the flask in his breast pocket. A Yankee artillery round lands on a South Carolinian, and all that's left lies in a crumpled pile of clothing. A frozen bolt of fear hits Clay as he imagines himself a pile of crumpled clothing. Duty calls him back to order.

"Sergeant, check the men," the lieutenant orders as he takes a long draw from his flask.

"Yes, sir."

"Shoot any deserters, Sergeant!" Lee slurs.

Clay moves behind the company to check cartridge boxes and cap pouches. "Keep your alignment." He inspects.

"If a man gets hit, let him go back to the aid station on his own." He wonders what Stewart thought about when he inspected the men. Clay comes upon Barnabus, his shaking hands struggling to open his cartridge box. Did George feel sympathy for human weakness? Clay can't, for to him, weakness is a monster, a monster Clay's battled since this journey began, and nothing can make a man feel more powerful than standing up to the personification of what he does not want to ever be again. Clay opens the cartridge box.

"Stay close to Perry and me. Do exactly as you're told, and you'll do fine."

"I don't want to die in this one," Barnabus says.

General Anderson rides to the front of the company as Clay continues the inspection. Seeing Anderson gives Clay even more military bearing. Clay checks Neil for cartridges. General Anderson halts his horse just in front of Lieutenant Lee where he inspects his brigade.

Clay feels the thunder of hooves announcing more riders approaching. A gilded rider calls to Clay's general, "General Anderson."

"General Buckner."

"General Anderson, may I introduce General Longstreet?"

Longstreet! Clay looks up to see General Longstreet offer a handshake to General Anderson, "General, what men do you have here?"

"Mississippians, sir, and the finest stock of men in any

army," Anderson boasts then states their brigade moniker with pride, "High Pressure Brigade, sir."

With a nod of approval, Longstreet inspects the troops. Clay's mind searches for a way to get his attention. He thinks about asking for more bacon. *How stupid would that sound?* Better to be invisible than embarrassed. Clay returns to his inspection.

"General Anderson, I have Mississippians in my corps. There is no equal." Longstreet says. Clay feels Longstreet's eyes upon him. "And it looks like your men are cut from the same cloth." Longstreet recognizes Clay. "How was that bacon, sergeant?"

Neil looks to Clay.

"Excellent, General. How were the sweet taters?"

Longstreet offers a deep laugh. "Best I've had in years." He pulls himself up in his saddle like a preacher about to give benediction, "It would appear I'm the one to join your unit, sergeant."

"Glad to have you with us, sir," Clay begins to feel the equal of any man.

"We'll attack hell itself if you order it," General Anderson interjects loud enough for his men to hear.

Duty calls Longstreet away as Company D feels the sting of an artillery round; two men become grease spots.

"Sergeant Miller."

Clay snaps around to Lieutenant Lee who, wiping his mouth, asks, "What time is it?"

"Don't have a watch, sir."

"Get one, damn it." Lee takes a deep draw from his flask.

"Yes, sir," Clay agrees.

"Attention battalion. Forward, guide center," the colonel orders.

Clay sternly reminds everyone, "Any wounded man must show me red before I'll let him leave the line."

The sober colonel flourishes his sword, his horse prodded to two legs. Pure theatre, but it gives the boys goosebumps.

"March!" Drums pound. Left feet step out. The advance begins.

Moving across a road, they enter a large corn field. The regimental flag picks up the breeze. The pop, pop, pop of Manigault's skirmishers intensifies at the moment. Manigault will be fully engaged soon. To the right, General Deas' Brigade moves as if on parade. Smoke erupts from across that field. Individual Alabamians fall. Clay looks to Barnabus tripping more than marching, stumbling more than attacking. Over the lieutenant's shoulder, Clay sees Manigault's lines stop. Their muskets rise in one smooth motion. Their guns go to their faces. The peeling roar of their brigade volley hits the heart like a drum, and in seconds smoke obliterates them from view. A minnie ball whizzes past. In spite of his marrow deep fear, Barnabus gawks at a spectacle no book or imagination can create. He's never seen anything like this before. Clay once watched battle like it was a circus, but Shiloh stopped that foolishness.

The colonel yells, "Lie Down," and regiment drops as one and will stay down until Manigault has broken the line, or dies.

His head by the lieutenant's feet, Clay feels the bullets buzz over. Lee kicks in spasms every time one gets close. The colonel rides up.

"Lieutenant Lee, are you injured?"

He raises slightly, "No, sir. The orders were to lie down."

"Yes, they were," the colonel resigns himself to having a coward in his officer corps. He rides down the line, past the standing officers of the other companies.

A Yankee bullet clips a thistle, the needled leaves falling on Barnabus. He buries his face in the red Georgia dirt.

Across the field, line after line of confederates advance. Clay waits to see them melt under the heat of a Yankee volley. Their pace quickens. The roar of musketry should be deafening, yet he hears only a smattering of shots. Nothing like Murfreesboro.

"Rise Up," is commanded, and Clay's unit advances. Manigault's not dead, and by the pace of his advance, he's not being challenged. This field of death lies unplanted. It appears to Clay that Rosecrans is up the spout and the boys can sense it. The stream of wounded is nearly absent; only the frenzied pleas of a few demoralized blues surrendering shows any sort of battle here. Passing the regiment, a courier yells, "We got em good. They ain't in our front." Manigault continues his advance, and so does Clay's brigade.

Across a well-worn road, then up a small berm, through another field, and into a woodlot, the 7th struggles to maintain their line as trees and undergrowth tear at the uniformity so vainly pursued by officers and NCOs. Positioned on the far right of the brigade, the 7th feels fire on its flank. A battery of Yankee artillery shreds the trees above the regiment, showering Clay's company with deadly splinters. Private Cobb falls. Clay goes to him.

"Son of a Bitch!" Cobb's hand steadies a branch that's imbedded in his right eye. "Gonna lose an eye?" Cobb snaps.

Clay nods. "Yup."

"This means I'm done, don't it?"

Clay understands the question. "I believe so. Can't trust a one-eyed man with a musket."

Cobb smiles.

"Can you make it back by yourself?"

"Hell-fire, boy. I'm halfway there," Cobb is up and moving quickly for the rear.

The forest darkens as the regiment gets deeper under its canopy. Mounted officers fight branches that threaten to dethrone them.

Lieutenant Lee tosses his squeak into the chaos, "Keep up, you lazy shits. Cowards, damn ya. Keep up or I'll shoot you myself."

Perry slows to step over a wounded man begging for help, and for it, he feels Lee's wrath. The lieutenant hits him with the pommel of his sword. Something inside tells

Clay to duck just as the blade swishes past his already scarred cheek.

"Watch the damn sword," Clay yells out before he has a chance to censor himself.

Lee raps Perry again. The regiment slows as they near a high farmer's wall that separates a plowed field from a woodlot. As Perry begins to climb, Lee follows close. Clay looks down the line to see how the company is doing. Well worn shoes slip on the irregular jumble of rocks when he hears his name.

"Miller!"

Clay looks down to the fallen lieutenant, red faced and holding a small rip in his pants. The company stops to see Perry standing over the lieutenant.

"He slipped on that rock," Perry calls out to those around him.

"You lying son of a bitch, you pushed me." Lee searches frantically for his sword. "I'll kill you! I'll kill you!" his bloodied voice cries. "Look what you did," he points to the rip.

"Sergeant! Shoot that bastard!"

The order shocks Clay.

"Do you hear me? Bayonet him! Shoot him! Kill him! That is an order. Do you hear me? An order!"

Not long ago this would be a crossroads moment for Clay; whether to cow to a tyrant or to stand up to him. The entire company stays to see the show. Not today.

"Look what he did to me. Look at me, sergeant!"

Suddenly up comes a frothing horse of the colonel.

"What's going on here?" the colonel looks at the lieutenant, and then to the rest.

"Sir, I was shoved to the rocks by this man," pointing to Perry. "I want him shot."

Perry stands quiet.

Lee looks to the colonel for support. "Shoved I tell you. Shoved me down. Wanted to hurt me."

Clay stands up, "You tripped, lieutenant. That's all."

Forgetting his knee, Lee rises, but before anything can happen, the colonel ends the scene.

"Lieutenant, it's time for you to act the officer. Now, sir, get your company back into line." The colonel turns to Clay, "And you, sergeant, I expected better of you." Turning back to the lieutenant, the colonel orders, "Now catch up with the regiment."

"Sir, my leg."

"Very well," The colonel tells Clay, "You take the company back in line." The colonel returns to Lee, "Lieutenant, get along as best you can." And the colonel is off to more pressing events.

Clay forms the company and leads them back in line while Lieutenant Lee limps just fast enough to fall behind.

No longer the reserve, General Anderson orders his brigade to wheel right and go after a Yankee battery sitting at the bottom of a rise.

Advancing, Clay's brigade moves to within eighty yards of the booming guns. Ordered to move at double quick, their formation begins to lose its linear veneer. The 44th Mississippi moves ahead of 7th. It's now a race Clay wants to win. He wants to see crossed cannons on the flag of the 7th.

Seventy yards. The battery has seen the attack, their officer frantically orders his guns to action left.

Sixty yards. The gun's Number Five man brings a round of canister to the barrel—twenty-seven iron balls built to leave nothing but cloth and mangled bone. The barrels have found the 7th. Clay sprints for his life.

Fifty yards. The Number Two man feeds the barrel with two rounds of canister—fifty-six lead balls will vaporize everyone it its front.

Forty yards. Ramrod removed.

"Battalion Halt!" the colonel belches.

No time to dress the line. *Hurry, damned it, hurry.* The Number Four man puts the friction primer in the vent. Stepping back, the Yankee looks to the gun captain for permission to pull the lanyard.

Clay takes aim at the chest of the man with the lanyard. Clay kills a man today.

"CHARGE!"

The bayonet. Yankee artillerymen, not equipped for hand-to-hand fighting, pitch in using buckets and swabs in their futile attempt to save their guns. In a matter of moments six Yankee cannons sit quiet. Facing Hiram and Neil sits a still loaded cannon. Clay races past the barrel to the lanyard, now loose in the hands of a dead man.

Pulling the lanyard free, he makes the cannon inert. Clay gulps air. Taking a deep, purposeful breath, he holds it for a long moment then allows it to escape out of his mouth. The moment slows, giving Clay time to look at a dead federal at his feet. The lanyard still lays across his chest. He has a large hole in the center of his grimy forehead. His Yankee eyes fixed. Clay, Realizing what he did this day, feels bile build up and about to erupt when a horse's agony distracts him. A lead artillery horse struggles to get out of the harnesses that ties him to the limber and his five dead teammates. Tripping on his dangling forefoot, he cries out every time he tries to stand on the mangled limb. A sympathetic officer pulls his side-arm followed by a moment of silence as the pained horse stares into the black eye of the colt revolver. A shot and he goes down screaming. The horse dies fighting death until the end. Clay killed a man today. He had a man in his sights and he pulled the trigger.

"Sergeant Miller."

"Yes, colonel."

"Well done, my man. You saved a lot of men," the colonel beams. Excellent shot. Now son, reform the company so we can get after those Yankee devils," the colonel orders loud enough for just-arriving Lieutenant Lee to hear, "Only wish I could give you the company, but rank matters." He turns to Lieutenant Lee. "He deserves it more than you."

Turning to the regiment, Clay gets his boys back in

the fight, "Battalion. Change fronts forward on the last company. Battalion left half wheel," the colonel fights the sound of battle.

"March."

Checking the alignment of the company, Clay sees a body drop to the ground. It's Private Sermon clutching one thigh then the next. Clay checks on him.

"Sermon." Clay sees the ground meat and chunks of bone that tells that Sermon will lose both legs.

"Stretcher bearers will be by directly."

Clay leaves the fading sound of Sermon's violent praying, "O see my affliction, and rescue me."

"Battalion Ready."

Clay looks to Barnabus Lazerus. Still with the company.

"AIM."

Barnabus brings musket to cheek. He closes his eyes

"FIRE!" He pulls the trigger.

"LOAD!"

Muskets come down, fingers pull paper bound rounds from cartridge boxes. Front teeth tear at the cartridge tail. Barnabus bites too far down the cartridge, filling his mouth with gunpowder and gagging on the mixture of saltpeter, sulfur, and charcoal. Clay grabs the musket and loads it for him.

"Bite only down to the fold of the tail then pour the gunpowder down the barrel."

Clay tries to instruct a man more caught up in cleansing his mouth than learning how to fight. Many a coward has knocked out his front teeth. Without front teeth, a soldier can't tear the paper cartridge. Without front teeth a soldier can't be a soldier. Clay is surprised Barnabus hasn't taken that route.

Returning the musket, Clay orders, "Shoot straight."

"FIRE!"

"Reload!"

Ramrods smack into each other as the intricate ballet of loading is made cacophonic by jostling of men trying to avoid Yankee lead. Round after round is driven down the barrel by ramrods spun on high though the air, shoved down the barrel then returned to their position. Clay watches as Hiram pulls his ramrod from its keep, spinning it in the air with practiced skill, then, at midpoint, swings it just off to the left so it lands square on Neil's head.

"Hey, cut that shit out," Neil turns to confront Hiram, but before a row begins, Clay swoops in, "Neil, get back to your piece, damn you."

Hiram smiles and fires.

The muskets are beginning to foul from the residual powder left from a dozen explosions. Barnabus returns his musket to the ground and begins loading. His front teeth are black from the gunpowder he continues to eat with every tail he tears off. *At least he's fighting,* Clay thinks to himself.

Firing continues until the colonel orders a cease fire. Then silence. Tension questions the silence then, from somewhere, a wag yells out, "Yanks done skedaddled," and the regiment sighs relief. Skirmishers put out, exhausted

Mississippians catch their breath and count their blessings. Tension dissipates like the smoke on a battlefield. Men speak in hushed tones for fear of starting something.

Clay inspects his clothing. A bullet has punctured his new jacket, but not him. Reaching a blind hand into his haversack, he pulls out the old poke sack. It too has a hole in it. Opening the poke, he pulls out his notebook, a Yankee bullet embedded halfway through. Transcendentalism has saved his life. Clay offers his first prayer of thank you. For his mother who did her best. For Alex who came to his rescue. For Hiram who sparked the light of thought. For Julie. For Frank. For a notebook of ideas. In a moment of clarity, Clay takes a long breath. A faint smile comes across his face. When a bone breaks, it heals stronger at the break. Clay is stronger at the break. Life. For the next few moments Clay is a man loving life.

"Sergeant Miller."

It's Lieutenant Lee. Battle has made him sober and a bit more humble. He stands over a captured Yankee sergeant major. Clay moves toward them.

"You still need a watch?" Lee points to a watch fob attached to a blue vest.

"Yes, sir."

Lee pulls Clay's new watch by the fob made of the dark brown hair of the Yankee's wife. In no position to resist, the sergeant major watches Clay read the inscription.

"Forever, ninety-one years, nineteen days, and a minute. Love, Linda."

"What time is it, Sergeant Miller?"

"12:15."

About to sit down, he notices Barnabus violently whipping the ground with his ramrod.

Moving to him, "Let me see that ramrod," Clay orders.

Clay grabs the bent ramrod and forces it down the barrel of Barnabus' musket. "Must be three for four rounds stuck up in here. You can't fire it now."

Clay's more proud than upset with Barnabus. He challenged his natural instincts by toeing the mark.

"I wanna go home," he cries.

"Not yet," duty speaks for Clay. He begins searching for a replacement musket.

Moving to a collection of three dead federals; two who, in the act of carrying the third, were killed together, Clay grabs a Springfield musket. He checks its condition. It works. As he is about to return to Barnabus, Clay sees, off to the left, a mess of confederate officers laying hands on a dead Yankee general. Clay knows that many of these generals served together before the war. The dead Yankee must be one of them. He watches as tears flow from his general, tears of humanity. Tears of grief. Just moments before Anderson was pushing to kill every Yank in this field, and it was nearly done. In a real sense, Anderson killed his friend, and now he's crying over the loss. Clay turns to see a half kneeling Barnabus streaming tears of fear. While the rest of the company sleeps in this moment of peace, Clay Miller walks up to Barnabus Lazerus.

"Look up," Clay firmly orders in a voice meant to sooth.
Barnabus begins to rise up as best he can.
"No. Stay there. Just look at me is all."
His chest heaves as he fights to catch a breath.
Clay uses the musket to smash out teeth.
"Battalion, Fall in."
The brigade marches toward battle while Barnabus moves to the hospital then home.

Chapter Twenty-Two

September 20th, 1863

Night. Wiping the grime from his sweat-stained face, Clay is surprised how hot a cold day can get. Before him, the leftover men of the company do their best to fall in for a macabre post battle tradition established by the army in order to tally the butcher's bill. Roll Call. The shortness of the line and the perforated uniforms of the survivors tell of a victorious fight, a deadly fight, a fight ended unlike their other battles. For Clay, killing a man has made a painted battle on a flag empty. He's tired, but duty will not allow sleep.

Since no one has seen Lee since the final attack up that hill, Clay is in command of the company. Exhausted himself, he straightens his sore shoulders back in a struggling attempt to look more leaderlike than he's feeling. Reaching into his inside breast pocket, he pulls out his orderly book. Turning to this morning's roll call, he sees twenty-three names.

"Now let's see what I have left," he says just loud

enough to be heard, too low to be understood. Clay notes
his word choice, 'I have left.' He is now responsible for
all of them. Just as quick, he feels embarrassed thinking
of the men as *his* men. No man is another's man. A man
is his own: Frank taught him that. Clearing his head, he
returns to his duty. He looks at the men standing before
him, men who fought with a pluck and roar that makes
Clay proud to stand in front of them. Clay decides he is
proud of himself as well. It was he who kept the company
in line as they crossed that open field, the one just before
the hill still painted Yankee blue. It was he who constantly
redressed the line, pushed the men forward and relayed
the colonel's orders. Yes, Clay helped lead the company
on three assaults up that big hill, the one the Yanks still
occupy—Snodgrass. Still, the company did the work. Yes,
they are his men.

"Attention to roll call," Sergeant Miller orders.

Corporal Perry begins the line, more concerned with
the proximity of a hole in the center of his hat than with his
business. Clay looks to the rest of the company and what he
sees tells him they will not stand well in the fight that will
surely come in the morning. Vacant eyes tell of men living
in themselves: glad, confused, or thankful for being alive
when so many are dead. These reflective times may be good
for the soul, and Clay has certainly lived in himself, but at
this moment Clay needs them to live with him.

The men won't like it. In fact, they will hate him for
what he is about to do, but Clay Miller is Sergeant Miller,

and Sergeant Miller needs to put the military back into this collection of survivors. The enormous complexity of command stands on Clay's shoulders. He doesn't wilt.

"Let's get this line right, damn it!" Surprised eyes look up. "Right dress!" Bodies close the gaps while dazed faces turn slightly to the right. He knows they're tired so he softens his stance just a bit.

"The sooner we get this done, the sooner we can take a rest." The logic works and the roll call begins.

"Adams, Bill."

"Here, Orderly."

"Algood, William."

"Here, Orderly."

"Current, Neil."

"Happier than a gopher in soft dirt, Clay."

Pure Neil. And Clay is glad to see that piece of shit is still with him. The Hogg Mess will continue.

"Cobb, Joe."

Perry speaks up, "Old Cobb got it early on."

Clay remembers—a stick embedded in his eye. Sergeant Miller draws a neat line through the name Joe Cobb. The roll call continues, each survivor offering a "Here, Orderly" and each silent moment tells of a man from Mississippi killed or wounded.

"Love, John."

Love had fallen back with the remainder of the company after that last attempt at the hill. Three times they attacked up a hill that would tire a hunter and his dog.

Three times, sheets of flame from hundreds of muskets missed him. During a lull in the firing, he fell.

"Show red." Clay ordered him, making sure he was wounded and not showing the white feather.

"I ain't shot," Love snapped, insulted by the need to show blood. "Twisted my ankle real bad, that's what I did, twisted it on some root."

"We need every musket. Can you keep going?" Clay almost begged.

Love's attempt to stand brought a tooth clenched yelp, ending in a fallen heap of pain. Clay left him alone on that field.

"Rushing, James."

Clay recalls him about to ram the next round home when, thwack, his wrist flopped limp. Rushing stared in disbelief as his wrist dangled like a drown worm on a wet hook. Tough son of a bitch, he tucked the hand inside his coat, took a pull of tobacco, and spit his way across the field to the aid station. Not a whimper nor complaint. Matter of fact.

"Sermon, Jonathon."

Clay wonders if Sermon wants to live without legs.

"Wells, Everett."

He fell like a dead fish. Splat. Clay watched the slight bounce then the body settling. He never made a sound.

"Spring, George."

Clay saw bone sticking out of Spring's ripped sleeve.

"Stringer, Hiram."

Silence.

"Stringer."

Silence.

Clay's eyes sprint from grimy face to bloody face trying to find his best friend.

"Where the hell is he?"

"Last I saw of him was after our first attack up the hill, near the top," Neil blurts.

Clay too remembers seeing Hiram near the front as they moved up that hill. The last he saw of him, Hiram's soldierly form continued loading and firing well after the company retired.

Neil asks, "Should we go after him?" a surprise question from a man who seemed at feud with Hiram.

Just then the major limps up. "How's' your company, sergeant?" his concerned inquiry is in contrast with the peckerwood they encountered back at Tullahoma.

"We have a lost man, sir. Just about to go search for him."

The major looks across the battlefield at the scores of bodies. A soft moment fills his face. A redness grows around his eyes.

He turns to Clay, "There will be no search for lost comrades. Sorry, fellas, but we need every man here. Got to push them off that hill in the morning." Looking around, he clears his throat of emotion, "Where's Lieutenant Lee?"

Sergeant Miller steps up, "Sir, he's gone. I have the company at this time."

"Very good, sergeant. The 9th has picket tonight, so you can rest your men after you send a detail to help Garrity resupply his guns."

"Can't they do that themselves? Clay says recognizing the voice inside him is challenging the shit.

Exhaustion ignores the insolence, the major responds, "They have orders to keep a harassing fire all night. They lost two men today. Send them two of yours."

Unable to criticize the value of the order, Clay attempts to protect his men, "The boys are very tired. Do you think one will do?

"Very good, sergeant. Be quick now. No distractions. We need those guns firing all night," the major says as he limps off to check the rest of his regiment. The colonel died early on leaving the major in charge.

The adrenaline of war excites every nerve and muscle, electrifying sinew, but when the last shot's fired, and the last order is given, men will emotionally, spiritually, and physically crash. Two of the men in front of Clay are almost asleep standing. Perry cries a silent cry. Clay knows what he has to do. *Sorry, Hiram, you'll have to wait.*

A solitary Clay moves alone toward the sound of cannon. In the darkness, he sees flashes through the trees. Artillery likes an open field of fire, and Garrity has found a nice clearing on the side of the ridge just below the Yankee hill. His four brass Napoleon cannons spit individually, their blasts illuminate their crews. Clay follows the sparking trail of the round through the sky.

"Load," comes the voice of Captain Garrity, the only man in the army who can foul the air bluer than a cannon. "Come on, you scrapings off the boot of an Irishman. Give it to em right in the ass, you lazy sons of Erin."

The men love the old man and will fire at the devil himself if ordered to do so. Boom! And another round sends Yankees to hell. Garrity's guns eat cannon balls like a fat man eats grits. Clay sees a line of soldiers feeding them from ordinance wagons set closer than they should be to waiting limbers. *Well, don't that beat all*, Clay thinks. *The major sent someone else to help Garrity.* Seeing Captain Smith's men moving ammunition like quick silver, Clay decides one more pair of hands won't do much good so he begins toward the hill when he hears a call. "Come to give us a hand," Garrity requests and Clay's duty says yes.

While the rest of his company sleeps, Clay collects an armload of round shot from the wagon sitting squarely within federal range. First trip. A round explodes thirty yards behind the wagon; mules bay and teamsters pray. Second trip. A round dissects the line of men feeding the gun. Third trip, and each one more nerve racking than the last. With each trip, Clay feels his odds of surviving growing worse.

"No time for caissons and limbers, lads. Bring them damned shells up to the cannon's mouth," Garrity decreases Clay's odds even more.

Angry at sacrificing himself for his company and angry that he's not searching for Hiram, Clay fires off a, "Shit" with each step. Shit on shitting. The shit of life shitting on him just when it's getting better. Deep in shit. Just shit! A round lands and two of Smith's men fall. Clay steps over them as best he can. Looking down he sees Milford lost half his face. *Justified shit,* Clay smiles.

Coming to the wagon, the teamster hands Clay two rounds, and again he's off toward the guns when he hears a whoosh fly over his head. His eyes follow behind him to a blast of light and heat that knocks him to the ground. A Yankee round finds the wagon Clay just left, and for the next few moments the sky is a display of exploding phantasmagoric light. Hugging the ground, Clay watches as men run helter-skelter in vain attempts to remove themselves from the firestorm. Bodies fly as canister and case shot wreak havoc. Suddenly, a shower of dirt pounds Clay's face as a round buries itself inches away. He waits to die. *It's my time,* he thinks. Thoughts of all the ways he has seen men die fills his mind. *Please make it painless*, Clay prays. Time slows. Sound disappears. Thought disappears. Fear fades. Clay feels the individual blades of grass touch his face. He feels a snake as it slithers past him. Clay's heart becomes a silent drummer. The light of the still exploding wagon glows in frozen yellow.

From somewhere deep in his intuitive soul, his desire to live sparks movement. *Better to die trying. 'Never quit' echoes through his soul.* A blast of hot air and particles pellet his back and neck like scores of bee stings. *I decide when I die,* his mind yells at the world. Clay's legs drive blindly into the night. He runs into the woods, where the darkened shadows of the cannon lit by the still exploding wagon tells him the thin distance between life and death is thick enough to keep him alive tonight.

"Holy shit!" his lungs explode. He repeats, "Holy shit," as he fights to regain his breath. His eyes wide with life. "Not today," he tells death.

Clay watches as Garrity's battery pulls out. The night grows quieter. Thoughts reenter Clay's head. *I am the transparent eyeball; I am nothing, I am all, the currents of the Universal Being circulate through me*, the line from Emerson has returned. For the second time in his life, he has become the transparent eyeball. The first time, while checking the pickets at Bridgeport, when the breeze flowed through him and his mind became one with the world. Now here. Clay analyzes the parallel, and how one moment borne from nature at its most beautiful can evoke the same nothing/allness as being in an explosion. Both times he felt completely alive. Alive in every nerve electrified. Thoughts of transcendentalism move to thoughts of Hiram.

Moving from the woods, Clay drives past sleepy eyed confederate pickets and into the vacuum between enemies. He moves past broken muskets and dead men, grass fires and burning military ephemera punctuating the darkness. Wounded crawl, backlit, their forms dragging up or down the hill depending on the color of their uniform. Off in the distance, a spasmodic series of bangs followed by a blood curdling scream tell of a dying man consumed by his exploding cartridge box. Clay listens to the screams hoping not to recognize Hiram's tones. Each body passed is a body checked. Each cold face is not Hiram and so it goes. Moving across the field, Clay begins his movement up the steep hill he already attacked three times. The number of dead and wounded bear testimony to the viciousness of the fight. Trying to recognize something familiar, Clay spies a large boulder up in the distance that he remembers. During their second attack, he made it that far before going to ground. It was where he loaded and fired his musket at an enemy barely twenty yards away. It was where he finally used his bayonet for its intended purpose. Moving toward the boulder he sees his bayonet still embedded in a blue uniform. He left it there knowing he would never cook on it again. Clay Miller silently stands next to the second man he knows he killed.

Looking back to where he's searched, Clay realizes the futility of it all. Too many bodies. Too many fragments of uniformed men for him to ever find Hiram. His mind imagines Hiram dead amongst the thistle. Taking a calming breath, Clay channels himself from thoughts to feelings. What does his intuition say? What does the Oversoul say about the connection between friends? Is Hiram dead or is he alive? Alive. Yet his mind intellectualizes the probability of Hiram's death. So many have died this day. Thought versus feeling, Clay looks to the dead Yankee with Clay's bayonet standing tall in his chest. Which is right and which is wrong? So many bodies checked. A tear forms. The loss grows in him. Memories of his wound, of his time in hospital. The pain. His chest begins to heave. First Frank, then Alex, now Hiram, a loneliness, like a cold winter wind, moves through Clay. Tears fall. Alone. Alone for the first time in his life. He's always felt alone, but now he is really alone. A battlefield sound disturbs the moment.

Rather than fall too deeply into this black well of grief, he returns to a survival habit he learned as a child. He goes cold. Wiping the tears from his face, he begins the movement to camp.

"Halt," comes a voice from behind a boulder barely ten yards away. "Who's out there?"

"Lost soul trying to find home," Clay responds quickly.

From behind the boulder, the silhouette of the Yankee picket rises to wave him up. Alone, with nothing to lose, he moves around the boulder, but stays in the darkness. There, a Yankee scans the darkness Clay just left.

"Get yourself to this side of this rock before the Johnnies put one in ya."

Behind the Yankee, a small fire heats a cup. Clay takes a deep smell. Coffee.

"Is that fire a good idea?" Clay takes in the aroma.

"Need coffee if I'm to stay awake all night."

"Sure smells good."

Keeping his eyes on his duty, the Yankee offers, "Take some."

Looking at the campfire glowing small, looking at

himself to see how Southern he looks, Clay wonders if his
blue uniform will pass as Yankee. Hoping it's too dark to
really see the difference in uniforms, he moves in. Quickly,
Clay has the scalding cup to his lips, sipping the molten
liquid. Rolling the coffee quickly around his mouth, he
bathes in the taste. His coldness warms.

"Just be sure to leave me some," the Yankee whispers,
still looking in Rebel direction.

Kindness begets kindness, he offers the last of
Longstreet's gift.

"Say, that's good bacon. Where'd you get that from?"

"A general gave it to me."

"You talked to a general. Well, ain't that fine." The Yank
sidles over a bit. "What regiment you with?"

Clay puts his hand on the hammer of his musket,
"What regiment you with?"

"22nd Michigan. Our first fight."

Clay pauses, then takes the ultimate leap of faith, "7th
Mississippi."

Hands grip their muskets. Two pair of eyes search for
the next move. To fight means death for one, and probably
both. Both are monuments to unknown soldiers on an
unknown side of a hill.

Finally, Clay offers, "No use killin' each other. We won't
change the war if we do."

Blue exhales, "Sure enough."

"May I have another sip of your coffee?"

"Mind if I have another bite of your bacon?"

For the next moments two men sit in a patch of peace. The campfire crackles. The coffee soothes. The bacon satisfies. The sounds of death lurking in the darkness lose their significance. Clay wonders if peace is a manufactured thing, or a natural occurrence happening when men least expect it.

"Hear that?" Clay listens to the slight rumble of movement up the hill.

"Hear what?" The Yank comes up from his bacon.

Clay hears the muffled sound of the Yankee Army. "Your army is retiring."

"Can't be?" the Yank questions.

"Trust me, I know the sound of an army retreating in the night, and that's it," Clay points uphill. "You better get up there and join em before they forget and leave you here."

Clay can see the conundrum playing out in the Yankee. Caught between duty and the truth, he doesn't know what to do. He decides, "No, can't do that. Gotta stay my post."

Clay rises carefully, "Put that fire out. I could see your silhouette plain as day."

"Thanks," the Yankee settles into his picket duty while his army marches away.

Returning to camp, Clay looks upon the sleeping forms of his company. Moving to his knapsack, he sees his blanket covering two men, their faces concealed. Clay pulls the blanket from their faces. A tear of joy falls.

Chapter Twenty-Three

November 15th, 1863

Clay warms his hands by the struggling fire, its life challenged by a cold drizzle.

"Mind if I sit?"

Clay opens his blanketed arm like a bird's wing and accepts his friend under it. Pulling the blanket over Hiram's shoulders, they sit quietly. After Chickamauga, they all feasted on food left in the haversacks of dead Yankees. The night after the battle Hiram ate stewed tomatoes from a can. After chasing the living Yankees to Chattanooga, Bragg's army mounted the hills surrounding the city. Perching cannon on every prominence, he pounded them with artillery. To Clay, the Yankees looked like fish in a barrel. Bragg even managed to close their supply lines and for the first time, Federal soldiers ate rats. Clay hoped for their second victory of the war. That was two months ago.

In October, the Yankees broke the siege, and since then their supply line has brought in food and more troops. Meanwhile Bragg refuses to let his army build shelters for he refuses to admit he's lost the initiative. He also hasn't allowed his army to build defenses like those they built at Tullahoma; Clay thinks Bragg doesn't want to admit he's on the defensive. Bragg's orders are—and have been—to be ready to move at an instant.

To make matters worse, Bragg has sent General Longstreet to Knoxville. Two divisions of Longstreet's soldiers marched past Clay. At one point, Longstreet rode past, his jaw set firm, and his eyes on the road. Clay offered a salute to a man not seeing him, along with a silent thank you. Later, a passing soldier thought Clay was of Longstreet's corps because of his uniform.

"Get in here, boy," the soldier called out, "or you'll be stuck with ole' scarecrow Bragg."

Proud of his jacket, Clay felt like he could fit among them. To march off and start again appealed to him, yet duty and friendship kept him with Bragg. He pulls the shivering Hiram closer.

Neil perches himself on a stump by the fire while two other men busying themselves skinning their supper. Delicate work, they surgically remove the pelt from their hand size meal. Finished, they run a ramrod through it. Looking for two bayonets, they ask Clay for his.

"I used it at Chickamauga."

Making due, they prop one end of the ramrod on the stump Neil sits on and the other on the only bayonet in the group. Clay watches Neil stare at the emaciated rodent like it's a Christmas ham. They haven't seen meat in two days. Clay can't remember the last time he saw a vegetable. Scurvied, Neil's gums are beginning to bleed.

Neil moves toward the fire, "Looks like even the rats are on half rations."

A flash of a skinning knife has Neil retreating back to his stump. Meanwhile, Clay feels his body sinking into starvation. Desperate to alleviate his plight, he attempts to manufacture peace. Once in the woods, once in a cannonade, he found the transcendental world. He tries to return. He tries to close his mind and open his soul. Hunger won't let him for it has grown deeper and angrier than ever before. The ravenous pain in his stomach and the cold attacking his limbs forces him to live in this world.

"Hiram."

"Yeah."

"When does life stop shitting on us?"

"Never."

In a world of darkness and disappointment, only Hiram has stayed an illumining force in Clay's life. His unflagging and unconditional friendship has been a beacon of light. Now, arthritic from sleeping on the ground, Hiram moves in groans and pains. He is disappearing before Clay's eyes. *Why bother?* Depression turns to resignation.

"Sergeant," comes a voice from behind the fire.

Clay stares at a fire that cannot warm him.

"Sergeant Miller!"

Clay comes out of his stupor to see the man calling him.

"Officer's call in five minutes," Sergeant Major Dix turns to leave.

"I'm not an officer," Clay turns back to the fire.

"Be on time," Dix orders.

Duty again slaps Clay. The company hasn't had an officer since Chickamauga, leaving Clay to do his best to take care of the men. He has gotten what rations he could for them. He tried to get them out of as many details as possible. He's done his duty to the best of his ability. Hiram shakes. Neil pulls at a loose tooth. Two men eat a rat. *Why bother.*

Empty inside, Clay wraps Hiram in the blanket then begins the slow walk to regimental headquarters.

"See why we ain't allowed to build shelter," Neil blurts. The rat men even eat the bones.

Passing four men sitting ass deep in mud playing euchre, Clay watches them tease each other's card playing. They remind Clay of the light that has attended every episode of his life. No matter how deep the mud, there was good. Alex's friendship. Julie. Frank. Escaping Highland. Healing. Recognition. Acceptance. Self-awareness. Responsibility. Friendship. Sometimes just a spark, but still the potential for a better life was in each and every episode. Soaked cold by the mud and the drizzle, the card players bet imaginary food: carrots trump beef, coffee and tea are bowers, Salt pork are aces, their spirited banter a foil to the mud they sit in. Clay warms just a bit to their making the best of their plight.

Walking the distance between his company camp and the regimental headquarters is a journey past men too stubborn, too loyal, or too stupid to quit the army. He recognizes he's one of them. It's wearing on him like a leather strap to a horse's back, rub by rub until the raw nerves burn.

He passes men hiding under Yankee rubber blankets captured at Chickamauga, rugs from home, and the remnants of blankets that have long ago lost their ability to keep out the cold. There is little canvas in the regiment. The only significant canvas is found in a cluster of stained tents that make up headquarters.

Clay arrives at the tent of the regiment's new colonel. Fresh from command of a town on the Mississippi coast where the hardships of war meant having to eat sea bass instead of salt pork, Colonel Mayson is fortyish and showing it in the lines of his brow and the paunch inside his uniform. A nervous sort with a fidget in his movements and voice, he stands next to Sergeant Major Dix. Dix signals for Clay to come to them.

"Sir," Clay salutes.

"Colonel, this is Sergeant Miller. He's has company E."

Mayson's not used to being around veteran soldiers, his response showing his discomfort with having a field command. "Gggood. Very good," he forces composure. "Sergeant Major Dix here tells me you're doing a fine job with your company. I agree with him. You will make a fine officer."

Officer? Light again sparks in the darkness. Cautious, Clay's mind swallows the idea of being an officer. He knows he can do the job. He has been for months. He also knows officers tend to be a different species from enlisted men, and he's still not sure where he fits in this world. Officer.

"Did you hear me, son?" the colonel stands closer. "Congratulations. Looks like the sergeant major will be saluting you from now on, hey? Hey." Happy with himself, the colonel gives a nod to Dix. "What say you, Mr. Dix, time to give this gentleman his salute?"

Crisply offered, the sergeant major gives Clay the first salute of his life. At Shiloh, Clay had feared Dix's icy stare. That was then. War has toughened Clay. Now, he reminds him a bit of Hightower.

"Now you return the salute," Mayson offers like a proud parent having just fathered an officer.

Clay takes a fresh breath then salutes.

"Lieutenant, run your company in a manner befitting this fine regiment, and you will improve your station by joining the gentlemen of this regiment," the colonel instructs.

All business, the sergeant major prods the colonel, "Colonel, some of the officers are into their cups. We need to give them their orders before they go completely to the bottle."

"Yes, sergeant major. Thank you. Have the bugler sound the call. I'll meet them by the regimental campfire."

They leave Clay Miller standing alone. *Officer? How will this turn out?* Clay tries to predict how this new chapter will turn out.

Dix's voice stops Clay from thinking. "Hadn't you better join them, sir? That's where you belong."

"For now."

Muddied shoes move toward the fire where captains and lieutenants have gathered. Although showing the wear of this campaign, the officers are considerably better dressed than Clay, each having a complete pair of shoes and uniforms free of patches. One officer, Captain Smith, is downright crisp, with gold braid adorning his sleeves and collar; he stands in contrast to the faded black wool tape of Clay's chevrons. Clay moves to his self-appointed place in the back of the group.

"Gentlemen," the colonel fortifies himself with a big draw of air, then begins his pontification. "We have trying news. It has been confirmed that more Yankee divisions are forming near Bridgeport. Grant's Yankees in Chattanooga have been resupplied, and it appears they intend to make a movement soon. They are receiving regular and complete rations. We, however, have gained little from the new policy. Remember, if any of your men bring in a recruit, your man will receive a forty-day furlough. So far, only three in this regiment have brought in recruits. Remind your men." Mayson turns to Dix, "What else is there, sergeant major?"

"Sir, rations."

"Oh yes, we have just received orders to reduce rations to one quarter beginning tomorrow." Clay spits. "Not to worry gentlemen, I'll have commissary find the officer's mess something more substantial."

"Here. Here," some of the officer's reply.

"Gentlemen, any questions or concerns?" Mayson asks.

The voice inside Clay speaks without permission, "What about shelters?" the voice comes deep from within him, "I'll lose the entire company to sickness if I don't get them out from this weather."

"Well, Lieutenant Miller," Colonel Mayson offers, a bit perturbed. "Oh, by the way, gentlemen, this is Lieutenant Miller. He'll be in command of Company E, if he passes the examination."

The crisp officer steps out, "Yes, colonel. This weather is taking its toll on my boys. We need to get them out of the elements before we lose many more."

"By chance, I just this morning received a general order for the men to build suitable habitation. Well then, we better see to it. How about two days excused duty so you can put up suitable shelters." He turns to Clay, "Will that do?"

"Better than nothing."

Dix barks, "Mind your place, sir. Colonel is doing his best."

Clay stands silent.

Mayson, not sure how to take Clay's insolence, asks, "What else do you need sergeant, I mean lieutenant?"

"Scurvy." Clay is beyond trying to transcend. "Scurvy. One of my men has scurvy. His teeth are beginning to fall out." Indignation amplifies Clay's tone, "What about that?"

Dix responds quickly and firmly, "Grass."

The well-dressed officer snipes, 'Grass! How can you suggest grass to men who have held with us through so much?" Captain Smith grows angry. "My boys deserve more than grass, damn it."

"Sir, boiled grass soup can belay some of the effects of scurvy." Dix explains, "Not a perfect remedy, but it will help until we can get proper vegetables to the men." Dix looks to the officers.

The colonel nods, meeting adjourned. Clay moves off alone. On the way back he plucks as much grass as he can find and stuffs it in his haversack. It appears some men have already fallen on the idea which forces him to search hard for something so basic.

Returning to camp, he sees Hiram and Neil sharing Clay's blanket. He puts a pot water on the fire.

"Grass soup for supper tonight."

Tomorrow Clay will get them in a shelter. An officer can get better food. *Maybe, just maybe.*

Chapter Twenty-Four

November 19th, 1863

The axe blade swings in its well-practiced path toward the newly scarred pine. Just before contact, Clay twists the blade, wood chips exploding from the gash made from the educated swing. Frank's lesson has a half-starved Clay knocking down trees like the youthful man he once was. Pried from the tree, the axe repeats its action; each repetition energizing his soul and firing his sinew. A line from Emerson fits the moment, *'In nature a man sheds his slough, for in nature is perpetual youth.'* Nature and labor have revived a man close to giving up. He again finds solace in the woods. It started two days ago when Clay and his mess found this patch of piney woods four miles from camp. Too far away to feel the destructive touch of the army, Clay found peace in the unbroken ground and untouched white pine. At first, he felt conflicted. So beautiful. So perfect. So untouched. A blanket of pine needles so soft underfoot, he was even reluctant to insult this spot with his boot print. Then the thought of the seventeen freezing men needing shelter removed Clay's reticence. *Nature renews itself. Only man dies and rots into wasted glop. This wood will return, by seed, once I'm gone*, Clay reminded himself.

His men's needs pushed the first swing. Hiram's and Neil's conditions pushed the second and third. In a self-serving moment, Clay earmarked the first logs for the Hogg Mess cabin. That night they built theirs nice and tight. Today, he and his pards provide wood for the rest of the company.

Clay moves across a small creek to get at a patch of stout pine while Neil strips branches from the already felled trees. His movements are weak and unstable, but he's doing it. Hiram loads the wagon, his arthritis making each log a battle of wills, but he does it.

"That boy's going to town," Neil grunts, struggling under the weight of a pine log he drags over to Hiram. "Need to take a break," he sits down. Hiram joins him. They watch Clay as makes quick work of another tree.

"He's a good man." Neil observes.

"Sure is." Hiram adds, "Too bad."

Curious, Neil asks, "Why too bad?"

"My father, Mr. Stringer, sent me to college to learn about 'the fabric of man,' as he called it. I joined the army for the same reason."

"What's that got to do with Clay being a better sort than just about anyone I ever met," Neil asks.

"Exactly."

Before Hiram can explain, the ramrod Sergeant Major

comes up. Dix seethes at seeing two men lazing about. He stops in front of Neil and Hiram. trying to find patience, he asks, "Instead of sitting about doing nothing, where is your lieutenant?"

Neil answers the slight by showing Dix his bleeding gums.

Dix softens, "While you're out here, grab some grass, roots and all. When you get back to camp, boil it to make a soup. That'll help. Did for me when I served in Mexico."

Neil points to Clay, "He brung us that couple a days ago." He tugs at another tooth. "Think its workin."

Moving toward Lieutenant Miller, Sergeant Major Dix sees Clay cutting down a tree, an act that completely disregards military decorum. Although Dix's old army mindset is disturbed by an officer doing manual labor, he finds the power and ease of the new lieutenant appealing. A lifetime enlisted man, Dix respects the rank, but his upbringing has him more akin to those like Miller, and in that Dix has decided this hickory knot will become the best officer in the regiment.

"Lieutenant Miller." Dix calls out. Clay stops, his serenity interrupted. "Colonel Mayson wants to see you."

In a moment of reflection Clay looks at the axe. "One last swing then I'll go," he tells him. One last time he gives that slight twist just before contact, just like Frank taught him.

Crossing the stream, Clay hands Hiram the axe then. "Try not to break this one."

Hiram smiles. Clay leaves the woods. Neil can smell his putrid breath.

Returning to camp, Clay smiles at the same four men still playing cards. Nearing the colonel's tent, the sergeant major escorts him in. Sitting behind a desk, Colonel Mayson accepts Clay's salute.

"All prospective officers must pass a written test," the colonel councils.

He hands the lieutenant a drill manual. Clay leafs through the hundreds of pages, each filled with pedantic text on school of the soldier, school of the company, and school of the battalion; all stuff Clay has performed for these last months.

"This will be an oral test given by officers of this brigade. It will be stringent," Mayson pauses. "Sorry, big word. I mean difficult."

"I went to college."

Surprised at the ragamuffin in front of him being college bred, Mayson approves. "Well then, you understand the," he pauses, "the—stringency—of this test is to ensure the regiment has only the finest officers leading it. If you pass the oral examination, then you will be evaluated on how well you drill a company. Then we'll see if you can apply the theory."

Clay stands silent and empty.

Mayson inspects Clay's uniform. "And I must say, if the way you dress is any indication of your respect for the position for which you're being groomed, well, I fear sergeant might be as high as you go in life."

"Yes, sir."

"Get yourself a proper uniform,"

"Where?"

Mayson recants, "At least remove those stripes."

Clay leaves the tent. Walking back to the cabin, he nods his head in a familiar disappointment, "And there it is." *Same old shit.*

Opening the canvas door Neil made from cloth found on a nearby wagon, Clay ducks into the Hogg Mess cabin. It's an excellent cabin, thanks to Neil's prewar skills as a carpenter. His creation holds three bunks against a side wall, each one barely two feet below the previous. A window of linseed oiled canvas provides the only source of light in this snug space. A table sits under the window, close to the fireplace and in the sun. Three chairs made from discarded ammunition boxes fill out the furniture. Gear and muskets hang from pegs bored into the wall opposite the smoldering fireplace. The cabin's pungent aromatics and roughhewn amenities belay its comfort. It is truly an improvement from the outdoor living they've endured since spring. Since moving indoors and being able to sleep on a warm dry surface, in a short time Hiram has regained some of his vigor by losing some of his pain. Neil's asleep in his bunk.

Where Waterford crystal once filled his hand, Hiram holds a wooden spoon. Coming up from his fireplace crouch, Hiram shows what the three have to live on today, "A pound of beef, a handful of cornmeal and half a blackening cabbage. Coffee's up."

Placing the drill manual on the table, Clay grabs a hot cup of sweet potato coffee.

Seeing the book, Hiram says, "Let me see that," and greedily snatches it. "A drill manual?"

"I have to take an oral examination."

"Not your strength, my friend."

"It gets better. After the examination, I have to take the company out for drill so Mayson can see I'm not an imbecile."

Taking a seat, Clay pulls his jacket off; then, opening his pocket knife, he begins taking off the stripes of his former post. Careful not to destroy their integrity, he gently cuts and pulls until only shadows of the rank darken his jacket sleeves. Six chevrons lie on the table. Perry will move up to sergeant, Clay will need to fill that corporal's spot.

"I need a corporal," Clay shows Hiram four stripes.

Hiram dumps the rations into the pot of boiling water. Silence fills the cabin, then, "You may need to find a candidate who will be here for the duration."

"Forty-day pass?" Clay offers.

"Those who take the furlough seldom come back. Still want me to take those stripes?"

The sun sets, the stew boils, Neil sleeps, Hiram sews chevrons, and Clay attacks the pages of the drill manual because he wants a better chapter. Taking page after page of Hiram's stationary, Clay draws out each maneuver then envisions each move, rechecks the text, then repeats the process. The mental exercise excites him like when he was back at school.

"If I pass, we can eat better."

"Not as good as this," Hiram doles out the muddy looking soup that smells as bad as it will no doubt taste.

"Never as good as this." Clay means it.

Chapter Twenty-Five

November 21st, 1863

As morning dawns dim over the eastern edge of Missionary Ridge, Clay's bloodshot eyes study *School of the Battalion* for the fourth time when he hears a knock on the cabin door. Quick to answer so his mates don't wake up, he finds a tall, lean Negro with a servant's eye looking up at him.

"Ishmael," he bows respectfully, "Massa Smith's nigger. Iz here to get Lutenant Milla."

Clay wonders why Smith sent his servant, "What do you want me for?"

Ishmael inspects the slovenly man in front of him, "Lutenant Milla?"

"I'm Lieutenant Miller," Clay feels the inspection.

"Sa, Massa Smith invites ya to breakfast and drill talk. Says brings da manial ifn's ya got one."

Captain Smith is the best dressed man in the regiment, maybe even the brigade, as is his company. He takes good care of his men, and even though some have called him a dandy, all call him brave. Since Shiloh he's led the Milford Rifles from the front. He's also a man living a charmed life. Smith has never seen so much as a nick this entire war. When the ammunition wagon feeding Garritty's battery blew up, Smith was only feet from it and nothing. Regardless of whether Smith is lucky or protected, he has been a captain since the beginning so Clay decides to take his help. Grabbing his tin cup, plate, and drill manual, Clay leaves silently.

Knocking on the wooden door of Captain Smith's cabin, a volley greeting hits Clay, "Well, well, if it isn't Lieutenant Miller. Come in, my man, come in."

Entering the well-appointed cabin, Clay sees a real table and chairs next to a bed with clean sheets. A sea chest sits at the foot of the bed. Near the fireplace, a genuine rocking chair sits cozy and warm.

"Mr. Miller, have a seat." In military parlance, an inferior must call a superior by their rank, while a superior may use the rank or the term 'mister.' Clay likes the sound of mister.

"Massa, should I get da meal now?"

"No, Ishmael. I want to get to know our new friend a bit before breakfast."

Clay's stomach cries out. Last night's stew was neither tasty, nor filling.

"Yessa."

"Lieutenant, care for a cup of coffee? It's real."

"Real coffee, not corn or potato peels?" Clay hasn't

tasted coffee since that Yankee picket.

"Ishmael, two cups of coffee. Sugar, Mr. Miller?"

Dumbfounded that, not thirty yards from his cabin, Clay witnesses the world of coffee and sugar. He's not sure whether to be angry, jealous, or impressed. He accepts the kindness.

Smith continues, "Two lumps, Ishmael." Clay hands over his tin cup.

Seeing the blackened finish of the dented vessel, sable hands offer a white porcelain replacement. The captain sports enthusiastically, "Coffee needs the proper home, and fire scarred tin will not do. CHEERS."

Clay accepts the cup, "Thank you, Ishmael." Turning to Smith, "*Moby Dick?*"

"Very good. Very good, indeed. No reason not to enjoy some culture in this world of barbarity."

His first chug allows too much flavor to disappear down his stomach. *Live in the moment*, he sips. Holding the coffee in his mouth, he swirls it around savoring each ounce. A gentle swallow then another sip, each one a mild intoxicant. A small transcendental moment in a cup of coffee.

"I see you removed your chevrons."

"Colonel's orders." Clay puts down the coffee. "Colonel Mayson wants me to look like an officer."

Smith directs Clay to a table and its chess set, "Join me, Lieutenant. If you don't mind, I thought we could go over some 'School of the Company' and 'School of the

Battalion,' using these chess pieces," Smith says as he picks up the white knight and hands it to Clay. "This is you." *The white knight.* Clay likes it, "I don't have a horse." Smith laughs, "Maybe after you make colonel. Let's get you to lieutenant first."

For the next two hours, Clay learns the technical aspects of the formations he has performed and studied a hundred times. Pawns become privates moving about the table, the knight positioning them according to the command. Smith watches their placement, offering corrections and praise accordingly. Clay enjoys the mind candy.

"Mr. Miller, battalion drill can be boiled down to three basic moves: flank, oblique, and turn. If I were to give the command, 'Close column in mass on the fourth company, right in front. Companies inward face,' what would you do?" Smith smiles, "Get this right, and we will have our breakfast."

Clay takes in a thoughtful sip of coffee. He had forgotten about food until its mention. Closing his eyes, he visualizes the movement then looks at the chess pieces. He catches the trick question Smith has embedded, "What company am I?"

"Very good, Mr. Miller. Let's make you first company."

"First company. Okay." Clay accepts the test. "Company, left face. Break two files to the front. Forward march. By files left. Halt. Front. Left dress. Front."

"Well done, sir. Well done, indeed. You are a good student," Smith beams. "Hungry?"

The ever-present hunger pains of a confederate had disappeared until Smith's mention of food. "I am a bit hungry," Clay offers a restrained reply.

"Ishmael!"

The black man sprints inside, "Yessa."

"Bring breakfast." Returning to Clay, Smith asks, "Well done, Lieutenant Miller. When is your examination?"

"Today, after last formation," Clay finishes his coffee. "Not sure when they evaluate my drill."

"Drill? Never heard of that before." Smith looks Clay up and down, then remarks, "Mayson is more impressed with gold leaf than oak so I can see him doubting your timber." He gets up and moves to the sea chest where he pulls out an Irish linen shirt, pants with a strip of gold braid down the hem, blue grey frock coat with gold ornamentation fitting a lieutenant's position, and a gold braided kepi. Clay has never seen one man own so much clothing. Smith hands Clay the uniform. Not one of Smith's fanciest suits, but beautiful just the same.

"We look to be the same size. Try it," Smith says.

If Clay accepts, they will be the nicest he has ever worn. If he accepts them, he will entering a new world.

"What will you wear?"

Pointing to the sea chest, the captain laughs, "I have even more uniforms at home ready to be sent if I need them," he says pushing the clean uniform into Clay's hands. "I haven't worn that since I was a lieutenant, and I have no plans on reducing rank, so take it."

Clay is becoming more comfortable with kindness, warming to it, even believing he deserves it.

"Now all you'll need is a sword and belt." He looks down at the rags wrapped around Clay's footwear, "And shoes." Smith smiles.

Returning to breakfast the two talk about drill, the regiment, and the upcoming battle they both know is coming sooner than later. When the last rasher of bacon is gone, and the last drop of coffee quaffed, they sit in food bliss. The silence of the moment slows time and space. Clay sits in silent transparency. His stomach is full, his mind is full, his soul is full. Clay watches Smith look out the window to a place far beyond what surrounds him. Lost somewhere. Clay sees two biscuits uneaten. He remembers Hiram and Neil.

"Mind if I take a biscuit for my messmates?"

"Take two."

They exchange warm handshakes, and then Clay returns to his empty cabin. The company is on picket. Shoving the clothes under his blanket so no one sees it until he's earned it, he sprints to the picket line where, for the rest of the day, he lets Perry run the company so he can continue studying the manual. Hiram and Neil munch on biscuits.

Chapter Twenty-Six

November 21st, 1863

At the last formation of the day the entire regiment stands erect on the drill field. Clay stands in the position of the officer as the order to dismiss is given.

Dix collects Clay. "At least you took them stripes off."

"Gotta look the part, don't I, sergeant major?" Clay pokes at Dix just a bit. "I have a surprise for you. I think you'll like what you see tomorrow."

"Yes, sir." Dix responds like a soldier who has seen everything, and thus is impressed by nothing anymore.

They go to brigade headquarters where Colonel Mayson, Clay's brigade commander, and some staff members will grill Clay on the minutia of the manual. Sergeant Major Dix stops at the tent flap.

"Good luck, lieutenant."

"Not coming in?"

"I'll be listening from out here," he offers with a nod.

Clay enters, and the examination begins.

"What is the distance between two ranks?" an officer asks.

"Thirteen inches, sir."

Colonel Tucker questions, "What is the object of throwing forward skirmishers?"

"Sir, to find and initiate contact with the enemy. To act as an early warning of enemy attack, and," Clay stumbles for a moment. He knows how to deploy skirmishers, but his mind goes blank. Suddenly he says, "to counter the activities of enemy skirmishers."

"Very good."

The examination goes on for two hours. From how the color guard is formed to how to take a column of companies and deploy them to the rear, he responds to each question confidently and correctly. Whenever the officers confer about the next question, Clay's mind wanders to the new uniform and what it represents. *Clay Miller an officer. How grand that would be,* he thinks to himself. He wants this. He wants this for himself. And then, not something he has often said, he declares, *I deserve this.*

Colonel Mayson finishes the exam. "Mr. Miller, this completes the oral portion of the examination. Tomorrow morning, I will attend a company drill led by you. Let's say, 7:00. Put your company through a series of commands of your choosing, and we'll see how you do."

"Yes, sir."

Clay leaves the tent past a proud sergeant major.

Clay spends the rest of the day in a quiet cabin reviewing school of the company while Neil and Hiram find someplace else to go so their messmate can concentrate. Before Neil leaves, he offers his mate a sip from the canteen, then laughed as Clay choked on the sting of bad whiskey.

November 22nd, 1863

Clay looks out the door of his cabin to a steady drizzle which has turned the drill field in to a quagmire. In the middle of the field he sees the company clustered about trying to stay dry. A pang of guilt overtakes him as he thinks about putting the men into that for his benefit. Still, he needs to today to be about him. Pulling the new uniform from beneath his blanket, he replaces the shirt he's worn since March with clean Irish linen. The freshness caresses his skin. Next, the cadet grey pants. Lastly, he exchanges a sergeant's kit for an officer's station- nine matching brass buttons shining as luminous as the gold braid on the sleeves and each collar. This is the uniform of a lieutenant and it fits perfectly. The sword belt, brought over by Ishmael last night, and gold festooned kepi finishes Clay's transformation from enlisted to officer. The shoes Smith gave him are way too small so Clay must continue in his old pair. Not perfect, but not bad. Clay Miller looks and feels like Lieutenant Miller, the commanding officer of Company E, 7th Mississippi Infantry. He heads out to what he is sure will be the easiest part of the examination.

Moving to the drill field, mud pulls a shoe off his foot. "What the hell?" He retrieves the shoe and in attempting to tie it tighter to his foot, he breaks a shoestring. He looks to see if the company sees him. They are too busy staying warm to notice the awkwardness of a freshly dressed officer in the mud. It's here he notices how quickly mud has attached itself to his pant legs.

"Nothing stays nice in this shithole."

At least the mud will hide his shoes, he thinks as he comes upon the gaggle of company men, grumbling about drill. He hears them, and for that, for them, he decides to do just three commands instead of the six he had planned. The compromise is as good as he can do for an apology.

"Perry," Clay calls out.

Perry pulls his tucked head from his collar to see the gild on Clay's new uniform. "Lieutenant?"

"Congratulations, you're now orderly sergeant." The company stares at Lieutenant Miller. "Fall the men in."

"What the..." is all Perry can get out before the company begins its movement into line.

"Lookie that?" Neil chimes in as he moves next to Corporal Stringer. "Night before our boy Miller was like us, and now look." Neil winks at his messmate.

"Bet he ate better than us last night," comes a voice from the ranks.

Hiram lets the boys know Clay's rations last night still sucked ass as much as the rest, "Oh yes, that black cabbage and rotten meat was truly fit for a general."

Neil chimes in, "Can't think of any better than old Clay to lead us." Voices agree.

"Three cheers for Lieutenant Clay!" Hiram's blare is followed by hoots and hollers.

These chilled, soaked, cheering men humble Clay. In their eyes, he sees a genuine pride in him. And for that Clay will be forever grateful for the life he's led, for this journey has brought him to this moment. Without the pain, would the pride and pleasure of this moment had ever come to be?

"Best damned officer in the regiment," Neil yells above the hooting. A chorus of agreement.

"Best we've had," Perry rightfully sobers the cheer.

Adjusting his kepi, Clay asks for their help, "Last night I passed the officer's examination."

"Never a doubt," Hiram confirms.

"Today, they want to see if I can drill the company. That's why we're out here."

"Makes sense," Hiram continues supporting his friend.

"Attention Company," Perry commands. The men line up as if on parade. "Right dress." Eyes move crisply right, shoulders match shoulders just like the manual calls for. "Front." Perry offers a salute, "Sir, the company is formed."

"Thank you." Turning to the company, "I promise to make this as quick as possible."

"No, Clay," Hiram mentors one more time. "You do this right."

"Stay warm until the colonel gets here, then we'll start."

For the next twenty minutes, the western wind pelts the men while Clay's watch races well past the appointed time. Their uniforms are beginning to soak through. Clay sees their hands reddening from the cold. A cough comes from the rear rank. Clay looks around. No Mayson. Hiram turns up his collar. Water runs off the slouch hat of a rear rank man down the back of the front-rank man. One swears at the other.

Perry puts on his sergeant's voice, "Where's Mayson?"

Clay's company stands alone on a rain swept parade ground. "Shit."

"Maybe if we move around, it'll be warmer," Perry suggests. "Besides, we could use the practice."

"Attention Company," soaked men attempt to straighten their stance to Clay's orders. "Company Right Face," wet feet move. "Break two files to the front," The men know their jobs. "Forward." Aching bodies lean. "March."

Left feet step off together. Clay can see in the crispness of their movements that they are doing their best for him. The next command will establish a battle line.

"By company into line."

The company execute the maneuver perfectly. Clay looks toward headquarters. No Mayson.

"On the right by file into line," the company's willingness to help Clay has limits. They are still starved, poorly clothed, bone tired, and soaked to the skin. They begin to struggle. Still no colonel. In spite of the valiant effort of the company to keep sharp, the weather is winning. A cough worsens, yet all wait quietly for the next command. Hiram sneezes.

"Shit!"

"Company Halt. Order Arms. In Place, Rest," the company slumps. Taking another look around, Clay searches for the piece-of-shit who would leave them out here for no reason. The only figure, the growing form of Sergeant Major Dix, punctuates the moment.

"Lieutenant Miller," he salutes. "The colonel will be by directly."

More men cough. Rains soaks deep. Finally, the colonel rides up wearing a rain suit better than the one Hiram had at Shiloh. Pulling up to the company, Mayson looks at Clay like he's the one who called the colonel out of his warm bed. He stops in front of Clay and waits for a salute that will never come.

Feeling challenged, and not knowing what to do about it, Mayson changes the focus, "Bit of nastiness, this weather. Let's hurry this along before I catch a chill."

Clay looks around at the dirty canvas and log cabins of an army barely surviving. He looks at the flagpole at the edge of the parade ground, the flag of the Confederacy hanging limp. He looks at fleshy cheeks and cold nose of Colonel Mayson. How absurd this is. Finally, Clay looks to the men in the company, Highland men. Men he's known at a distance since he was young. Men he has known intimately since he left Highland. He looks at Neil, the lout he cares about. He stops at Hiram. Images of the man he met in college fills Clay's mind; the spark in his eyes, the confidence, and worldliness of his character. The best man Clay has ever met. Hiram sneezes violently.

"Shit!"

"What's that, lieutenant?" Mayson takes the word as a challenge to his authority, "Say that again and you'll be back where you started."

Perfect words to summarize the small men who have tormented his life.

"I said, SHIT!"Turning away from Mayson, Clay orders, "Corporal Stringer, kindly get a length of rope and bring it to me quick as you can." Hiram sprints off to the cabin.

Dix comes up to Clay and whispers in his ear, "I know what you're doing. Are you sure about this?"

Clay smiles, "Attention Company."The men straighten. "Neil, I need you for a bit. Sorry." Clay looks to the rest of the company, "Go get warm, boys." The men look about, unsure what's going on. "Company break ranks. March."

They look at Clay, then to the reddening face of Mayson, then to Dix. Hiram returns with the rope.

"Get to your cabins and get dry," Clay orders his company. They stick around to watch this.

"What is the meaning of this," A baffled colonel snaps.

Lieutenant Miller takes charge, "Stringer and Current, each of you grab an end of the rope. Stretch it between you." Clay stares directly into Mayson while speaking to his messmates, "You'll act as the company as I give the commands."

Voices from the company illustrates their seeing the knife Clay drives in Mayson's inflated position of artificial authority. They watch real authority stab at the smallness of man. Mayson fumes. The sergeant major smiles. The colonel gallops back to his tent.

Clay takes the rope from his friend, "Guess we'll not be needing the rope today. He turns to the company. "You all best get inside before you catch your death." They finally leave to whisper for the next few hours their analysis of the events just unfolded.

Dix interposes between Clay and the two men who refuse to leave their messmate's side. "You know, men have been arrested for much less?"

"And much worse," Clay remembers the spy and Asa.

"Indeed." Dix pulls his heels together, thrusts out his chest and gives Clay Miller a salute. "Well done, sir."

With a wink, Clay returns the salute then puts his arm around Hiram and Neil. "I'm in the mood for some sweet potato coffee." The three head to the cabin where a warm fire awaits.

Upon arriving at the cabin, they see a servant sent by Hiram's father. He hands over a satchel filled with sausage, cheese, and a bottle of brandy. For the rest of the day, as the rain falls on their canvas roof, the Hogg Mess lives in warm spirit: Neil romancing the bottle, Hiram reading a life changing letter from his father, and Clay warming his hands by over a fired fueled by a drill manual.

As the servant prepares to leave, Clay charges him with a task: to return the officer's uniform to Captain Smith along with a sincere thank you note folded into the coat pocket.

Chapter Twenty-Seven

November 25th, 1863

Men flail away at rock and dirt with bayonets, boards, and even their tin cups, anything that can move earth is used to create a defense. Yankee cannonballs explode along the ridge line where Clay has lived since September. A cabin explodes sending shards of wood into nearby men. Fingernails tear off as frantic hands dig deeper into Missionary Ridge. Clay and his regiment stand in the crosshairs of an irresistible Blue serge.

"Miller!"

Clay rises up from the log he's been notching with the only axe left in the regiment. Handing the axe to Perry, Clay rushes over to Dix and a tag along.

"What the hell are we doing?" Clay points to the slowly growing ditch. "The engineers have set this line wrong."

Dix tries to calm the moment, "I see you're wearing your Virginia jacket again." Dix addresses Clay, "Don't let the men see you frazzled, sir. Not good for their spirits."

Clay doesn't need a drill manual or officer's bars to see

the inevitable disaster awaiting his men. And this is not the time for pretentions. The men deserve the truth.

"I can't see the bottom of the ridge. We'll be lucky if we get a round off before they flood over us." Clay looks at his men's futile attempt to protect themselves. "Bragg sure Jimmy fucked us this time." Clay turns to walk away, "Same old shit!"

An explosion knocks all three to the earth. Then, after a long moment, Dix and Clay rise knowing they just missed a ride across the River Styx. Meanwhile a fifteen-year-old kid, scrounged up by Mr. Stringer, lies in the fetal position wishing he were back in the orphanage.

"Get up, boy," Dix grabs the kid by the collar. Handing him over to Clay, "This is O'Dell. Stringer's father sent him."

Clay looks down the line to where he sees Hiram digging. A nearby shell explodes almost on top of him. Searching to see if his friend has died would be bitter irony. Hiram emerges from the smoke, and Clay calls him over.

"That one almost made mother cry," Hiram quips.

Clay points to the spindly youth, "Would you like to meet what your father has done for you?"

"Oh my!" Hiram's face lights up with the look of a man about to be set free.

"Guess you're going to miss this one." Clay pats his friend on the back.

"Too bad Stringer's staying put," Dix's order sends

white heat through Clay's mind.

"No way!" Clay moves toward Dix like a man about to commit harm. "Hiram's leaving."

A blackened cannonball, its fuse glowing in the grey sky, lands amongst men working in the ditch. They wait for the blinding light, searing heat, and piercing of flesh. Nothing. A dud.

"Bragg ordered it. We need every man," Dix echoes an order given to him.

Clay scans the thin line of frantically digging men. He can see the seeds of a route as scattered soldiers, too scared or too smart to stay and fight, begin to leave the line. He knows this fight was lost long ago. He also knows only men of character, like Hiram, will stick to the end regardless of result.

"I know he's your friend, but we need him." Dix rationalizes.

Hiram begins walking to the ditch.

Dix interposes himself between Hiram and life, "Lieutenant, look me in the eye and tell me you will follow Bragg's orders."

Decision made, "Hiram." Clay calls out.

Hiram returns, "Yeah, Clay."

Clay puts his hands on Hiram's shoulders, "Looks like you're going home."

A cannon ball lands underneath the half-drunk major spitting him in half. Dix nods in agreement.

Dix moves out of the way, "One more musket won't

mean a hill of beans difference. Stringer, you best get
going before it's too late." Dix moves past the quivering
leftovers of the major to report to Mayson that the 7th is
about to fold.

Hiram turns to Clay, "Come with me. Nothing you can
do here."

Down the line, a desperate soldier takes a rock and
smashes his teeth out.

Taking a deep, resonant breath, Clay brings the words
of Emerson and Thoreau into this world. Clay looks down
at his shoes. *When you have worn out your shoes, the strength
of the sole leather has passed into the fibre of your body. Measure
health by the number of shoes worn out.* "I've worn out my
shoes."

"Clay, we've lived Dante." Another Yankee round
bedevils two more souls. "Transcendentalism has no
chance in this world."

Two friends shake hands, one thanking the other for
teaching him how to be, and the other proud to know him.
Clay moves back to the trench.

"Yes, it does!" Clay yells as loud as he can to a world at
war. "Yes, it does," he tells himself.

A shell fragment sprints past his ear. The thumping
concussion of an explosion hits his heart. Clay turns to
Hiram's replacement, "So far as a man thinks, he is free."
Clay misses his friend already. "Emerson."

"Na, my name is O'Dell, Timothy O'Dell."

"Of course." Clay takes O'Dell to Perry.

"Perry, where's the axe?"

"Broke handle."

"Of course, it is," resignation paints the words.

"What we gonna do about wood for shoring up the ditch," a frantic Perry questions.

Clay's mind, trained by war, responds, "Tear down the cabins."

"Yes, sir."

And with that, the Hogg Mess cabin becomes shoring for the ditch where O'Dell digs deeper. Clay too digs at the earth with the scarred and dented cup he bought in Corinth. It turns out all Clay ever wanted in life was peace. Today he finds it in moving earth with his cup. A crescendo of military noise calls Clay's attention to the ridgeline.

"What's that all about?" O'Dell's doesn't know the vocabulary of war.

Clay does, "We're next." He turns to his company, "Grab your muskets." Clay stands up behind the works. "Get ready men."

Suddenly a grey clad scarecrow crests the hill. Falling forward, he makes quick work of the forty-yard killing field between the ridge and Clay's line.

Hurdling the ditch, the scarecrow warns, "You ain't gonna to stop em." He disappears down the road.

A moment later, two more men scramble past with the same message, followed by more, then more, until a flood of fear passes Clay's ragged line. The confederate exodus from Missionary Ridge has begun. For reasons only the

Universal Being can define, so far Clay's men have held their position. They quietly wait for the command to fire.

"Fix bayonets" Clay orders, knowing that after one shot, the bayonet will be the only available weapon.

Perry, seeing Clay without one, suggests he uses a dead man's.

To be yourself in a world that is constantly trying to make you something else is the greatest accomplishment. "No."

An explosion ten feet behind the ditch sends a shower of earth on their living graves. O'Dell peers over the head wall.

"Get your head down," Perry shouts. O'Dell swats away the order like a fly. Suddenly a haggard form crests the hill. A shot rings out and the man falls.

"Got him," O'Dell cheers. The man slowly rises then stumbles forward, his grey uniform announces him as the last confederate to crest the ridge. The next uniform will be blue.

Life is frittered away by details. Clay reminds O'Dell to reload.

Dix runs up, "Lieutenant Miller."

Clay moves toward the split handle and abused blade. *I wanted to live deep and suck the marrow of life.*

Dix sees bayonets penetrate November. "The bayonet. Well played, sir," Dix commends then runs off to check on the rest of the regiment.

Clay runs his fingers along the axe blade. Scarred and dulled by the labors of life, the handle broken beyond repair, *when I came to die, I discovered that I had not lived.* A tear falls.

Clay buries the axe. "Peace."

A Yankee skirmish line crests the ridge. Mississippi muskets fire. Union men fall. O'Dell fires into the head of a man. The Yankees return fire. The quivering orphan falls next to Clay.

A second drove of Yankees attack the ditch. A red-haired confederate reloads faster than any man ever has, and just as he puts the percussion cap on, a Yankee bullet ends the effort. All along the line men grapple in individual death wrestles. A Yankee feels the bayonet. A son of Mississippi feels the butt of a musket spill his brains. Perry raises his hands in surrender, but today killing stops for no man.

Neil comes up, "What we gonna to do?"

Confederates and Yankees kill each other. A Yankee squad sees the Hogg Mess. Clay takes a long slow draft from his canteen. *What lies behind us and what lies before us are tiny matters compared to what lies within us.*

"Clay, what we goin to do?"

Clay offers Frank's life lesson, "You can give up." Perry tried to surrender. "You can run away," Neil quits the discussion and begins to run away. A bullet chases him down.

Clay lives Frank's third choice. From his battle torn haversack, Clay pulls out a small gold axe. Free of life's constraints, with free will, he pins it to his jacket.

"Or you can stand up."

A Yankee sergeant, yells out, "Its hog killin time boys." He orders his men to fire at the standing confederate with the faded Virginia jacket.

Somewhere on the road to anywhere but here, Hiram Stringer hears the rumble of battle behind him. He has a half hour head start.

To know even one life has breathed easier because you have lived. This is to have succeeded.

The End

Acknowledgements

The story within these pages began as transcribed letters from a Confederate soldier that served in the 7th Mississippi Infantry. Not particularly rich in detail, it was that lack of detail that inspired me to fill in the blanks. Taking the skeleton of timeframe and historical event from the letters, the story I share with you is a piece of fiction set in real places, at real times, with real historical consequences for the armies described within. Clay Miller is a complete figment of my imagination, as are his mates and those he meets on his journey. The major military figures are based on how historians have described them, with my pinch of creative license tossed in.

During the making of this piece, I was assisted and encouraged by some amazing human beings. They read early, ugly drafts, offered clear criticisms and applause where earned. They all made me take a long hard look at Clay's story in order to make it better. To all of you, I say thank you. I also have to thank the editor, Denise Guibord, who showed me that my Gremlin needed a lot of work before it could sound like a Mustang. Not sure I got it there, but it is better because of your support and effort. Thank you, Denise.

Brad Graham: My film father whose passion for history, film, and life inspired me to take a shot at writing a novel. The moment I stepped on your Antietam set, I found a creative world I didn't know existed. This book would never have happened if it weren't for that creative epiphany and the people I met while working on the project. Then to offer to read this piece, something you did like a historical surgeon, was humbling.

Jay Barrick: He was an early victim of this piece, offering to read an early draft, making clear and appropriate comments for me to follow as I worked to improve Clay's story.

Lance Herdegen and Evan Jones: For reading my book with the historian's eye and a storyteller's mind.

Barry Hesson: For telling me I'm almost there, and being right.

My family: Two teachers and a mother, thank you for sprinkling truth in your love for me.

CPSIA information can be obtained
at www.ICGtesting.com
Printed in the USA
FFHW02n0800061018
48715245-52768FF